Nations Unite Within Souls We Walk

By

Viisions Life Force Foundation

Bloomington, IN Milton Keynes, UK

AuthorHouse™
1663 Liberty Drive, Suite 200
Bloomington, IN 47403
www.authorhouse.com
Phone: 1-800-839-8640

AuthorHouse™ *UK Ltd.*
500 Avebury Boulevard
Central Milton Keynes, MK9 2BE
www.authorhouse.co.uk
Phone: 08001974150

© *2006 Viisions Life Force Foundation. All rights reserved.*

No part of this book may be reproduced, stored in a retrieval system, or transmitted by any means without the written permission of the author.

First published by AuthorHouse 6/5/2006

ISBN: 1-4259-2712-2 (sc)

Printed in the United States of America
Bloomington, Indiana

This book is printed on acid-free paper.

Nations Unite Within Souls We Walk
and
Whispers Of Wisdom

Spiritual Teachings and Passages
From
White Eagle And Warriors Of Old

Many blessings and love we send out
To our dearest beloved Father who shared
With us the love and tenderness given
From the very essence of his life.

Viisions Life Force Foundation

Registered Charity No. 1112598

All Words Spoken Throughout
Are Given To Enable Those
Who Choose To Believe In The Walkways Of
Peace And Harmony And To Understand In The
Beliefs Of Many Cultures.
Wisdom And Knowledge Shared
With All Who Touch The Pureness Given By
Mother Earth's Creations,
To Enable Life To Continue For All To Share In
The Joys Of
LOVE

White Eagle

Contents

Within Souls We Walk 1

Whispers Of Wisdom 74

For All My People
To Share
The Knowledge And The Wisdom I Bring

Kaleidoscope of many gifts travel beyond the lands known to each and everyone. Beside the ghost of many memories, doubts form pockets of coldness.

Many brief encounters of walkways open for those who wish to follow the candle of life, fade from within once shadows begin to form through own fears. Weaknesses of many flow through the veins that sustain the life of own self. Challenge own fears with understandings of those chosen to bring the true meanings of peace back to walk amongst all Nations around the world of today.

My prayers I offer to fall upon each and everyone. Whispers of many ancient ones flow upon the winds of time.

Shelter no coldness for coldness brings sorrows of many hurts. Trust, open the heart to forgiveness. Share amongst those who cross own pathways the true meaning of love. Understand the life that has been given, walk tall amongst own Nations.

Feel the pain and sorrows of many who pass the pathway chosen by own self. Give understandings to the hurts done by many. Lift the veils of sorrow. Give own understandings, share within the heart and soul wisdom of many teachings. Walk free upon the carpet of life. Place the hand upon the arm of the one who cries tears of sorrow. Many share pains but fail to understand the true meaning of the deeds done. Fulfil own desires of meaningful understandings by acknowledging the worth of own self.

I share much with many of my people of time past, beliefs of Mother Nature's blessings. Caress by the touch of the hand the one thing we all share together, the earth we all walk upon, the air that we share by breathing, the waters we cleanse and nourish to sustain life, the winds that blow free upon the plains of all Nations. These are given by Mother Nature for all to share.

The sacredness of the White Buffalo has been given upon the plains of all ancestors. Tribal acknowledgement of the sacredness and true beliefs opens the pathway for my people to walk upon and share the freedom of peace and harmony once more. Many Tribal Nations share in the belief of the White Buffalo. Wisdom Keeper's acknowledge the sacredness that surrounds the coming of the White Buffalo. Each Tribal Nation brings forth offerings of many prayers. Many drums beat as one throughout the lands. Many prayers offered share the same meanings.

My wish for my people throughout Nations of today is to unite and walk as one hand in hand to bring forth the true balance of peace and harmony. Sacredness of all my peoples prayers, beliefs join together and harmonize and bring forth the true spirit and heartbeat of all Nations.

I give my blessings to all those who wish to walk beside the ones who share the understandings of all teachings of peace and harmony.

White Buffalo Calf Woman

Brother to my people, Saviour to many Nations,

Open with me, walk beside all.

Offer own hand in peace. Challenge no meaning. Trust in all Spoken Truth.

Knowledge I give. Wisdom I share.

Open the mind, share amongst those, teach through visions shown.

Feel the wisdom I bring to enable walkways of harmony to balance Nature's forces.

Touch the heart and soul of those who walk within the shadows of darkness.

Radiate with the love and warmth I bring in peace.

Understand the hand I offer.

Search no more, wisdom I bring. Each Warrior bring forth meanings of the soul.

Tether no more. Wisdom Keepers unleash knowledge of old.

Aho!

White Eagle

Nations Unite

Within Souls We Walk

Wings Surround Many Nations Of Your World.

PLACE

Honour, Trust And Your Beliefs

Above Many Thoughts Of Coldness.

White Eagle

Healing Of The Souls

Wondrous new beginnings will evolve through time itself, Nature's defence will bring about new beginnings,

Watch all. Manifestations will spring from the core of Mother Earth's bleeding heart. Souls wander through time zones trying to give back peace and harmony.

Roots shallow beneath world's carpet. Nations weep through own self pity. Teachings of all hearts of true believers slowly bring forth openings for each and everyone to follow through doorways, given in the hope of Nations to walk within the love of those who retrace footsteps trodden in the lightness of the one we share between creeds. Many names known for the one Creator given. Share the words spoken with me through travellers of your world today.

White Eagle
Spoken From The Heart

Nations of my people weep many tears of sadness.

Within the tears that fall, we feel the hurts, the pains, the anguish that befalls all.

Weak energies from many form shadows of doubts.

We bring teachings of words spoken by many Warriors.

Each word spoken brings pureness of hearts.

Place your hand within the hand of others who cross within the pathway of your journey.

Touch from within those who doubt.

Judgement from within bears angers for which the vibrations of harmony begin to disperse amongst shadows.

Leave the deeds done by many.

Take hold and envelop the ones who have wronged within your arms of pureness.

Each wrong doing will unbalance the balance of the journeys to come if left as an injustice.

Piece together the true meanings of what has been written.

Peace My Brothers.

White Eagle

Friday 13th August 2004

Regarded as an unlucky day by many back home in England but not by Gerry, Paul and I for we had landed at Phoenix International Airport, thus completing the final chapter to our book Spoken Truth, only to begin making firm footprints for the sequel you are about to read.

After a few hours rest at the airport hotel we picked up our hire car and set off with more than a little anxiety for our journey to Flagstaff, Arizona where Bennie LeBeau was waiting for us. After an arduous journey we finally reached our destination, rapidly checked in at our Motel and made for Bennie's room to meet with him for the first time. Introductions quickly dispensed with, we all sat and Gerry began to tell him of the incredible happenings that started on 18th August 2003 leading us to eventually meet with him in the hope that he could help us complete what was being asked of us.

As soon as he had been put in the picture Gerry opened the treasured briefcase she had been guarding day and night for months and produced the many sketches and drawings given to her by the ancient Warriors. Studying them intently, he quietly gave his interpretations as he did so whilst we listened avidly, for at last we could begin to understand their true meanings. Finally, when he had looked at each and every one of them Gerry handed him a turquoise copy bound in turquoise ribbon of the book Spoken Truth presenting it to him with the words "For you Bennie, from The Warriors Of Old. They honour you Bennie as you have honoured them by choosing to dedicate the remainder of your life to spreading the meaning and need of peace and harmony for Mother Earth". Tears welled in his eyes as he opened it and intently read some of the words spoken by his great people of time past. After a while he told us we had delivered to him 'strong medicine' and asked us to meet with him later for a meal as he needed time to read the many hundreds of pages quietly by himself.

After several meetings with Bennie it was decided that Sunday 16th August (American time) was the day to begin our search for The Keeper Of Old frequently mentioned in Spoken Truth by The Warriors Of Old as the one chosen to receive the golden copy of the book bound with gold ribbon. Bennie told us he knew of a number of Elders and at his suggestion it was decided we would search out each and every one of them in the hope that Gerry would be guided to the chosen one. We were astounded when told our first visit would be to a Sioux Sacred Sun Dance where he would try and find someone to meet with us.

The journey was long but we arrived at the secret destination late in the afternoon where we sat quietly in the car on Bennie's instructions whilst he went off to meet with the Elders. Over an hour later he arrived back at the car with those whom he wanted us to meet with. Introductions were made and, still sitting in the car as it was by now raining, we showed a sample of the pictures but to no avail. We left the Sun Dance discreetly making our way back to Flagstaff with Bennie planning our schedule for Monday 17th August.

This began with an early start to Flagstaff University in the hope of finding a Navajo medicine man, a friend of Bennie's and also a teacher at the University. We traced him to a diner and joined him for an interesting and lively meal for he had an amazing sense of humour. Sadly, this lovely warm hearted man was not able to help us in our search so, breakfast over, we presented him with the traditional gift of tobacco and bade him farewell in the diner car park. Although having met briefly we all felt extremely honoured and were left hoping we would meet with him again one day.

As we waved our final farewell the grey overcast sky above us intermittently lit up as silent forked lightening caught our attention. Bennie explained as we watched the silver threads of energy reaching forcefully from the sky to the earth, the Indian belief that lightening is in fact Father Sky trying to repair Mother Earth's core at the points where she is crying out for help. Although we had never heard of this before in England, to us it simply made sense. As we stood in the car park Bennie pushed Gerry to reach into her memory box for any clues she might have been given to find The Keeper Of Old. I too tried to recall anything we might have missed but Gerry was able to tell him she was certain the man had one foot missing and she could feel his hands tremble. Her Spirit Guides became very agitated and several times she repeated their words she was hearing, "Bennie, you know who it is, you know who it is".

During this conversation Paul, leaning against our car quietly smoking a cigarette whilst watching the sky in fascination suddenly said, "Hey you guys, did you see that?" He started to explain in astonishment what he had just witnessed but at the very same time Gerry and I saw Bennie step back with a jolt and he said, "I know who it is, the Keeper Of Old is Grandfather Martinez. The Thunder Gods have spoken to me". Throwing our arms around Bennie we hugged him with relief only to hear Paul say in amazement that he had just witnessed three forks of lightening reach out behind Bennie, Gerry and myself at the very same time that Bennie realised who the chosen one was.

The four of us hugged each other but without further ado Bennie informed us we had to move on immediately for we had to firstly meet with the Grand Elder For The Council Of Spiritual Elders Of Mother Earth. Bemused, we listened as he informed us we would leave immediately for Grants, New Mexico and the Navajo Reservation collecting on the way a KFC and plenty of doughnuts to eat with this Navajo Elder at his home. Bennie called him on his mobile to ask permission for us to visit with him, it was given and we set off within minutes as if we were on a jaunt to our local town back home in England. Little did we realise the journey would take us many exhausting hours.

We arrived at dusk and were warmly welcomed into the Peace Keeper's home where Bennie explained our reason for seeking to meet with him. Gerry presented him with his turquoise copy of Spoken Truth as she had been told to do by The Warriors Of Old and once we had eaten he produced a draft of his next book asking me to read it aloud for all to hear, which I did. Our meeting went on for several hours, then we departed for the long return journey back to our Motel. Nevertheless, we had accomplished what had been asked of us all by The Warriors Of Old and Bennie reminded us of the following 'Thank you's always come from the heart and not from the tongue'.

Allowing us minimal sleeping time Bennie had us back on the road early on the morning of the 18th for he had gained permission for our meeting with Grandfather Martinez. This was to take place at Grandfather's home so we found ourselves making almost the final footstep of our twelve month journey to the much revered Turquoise Mountain, New Mexico.

For this journey it was decided that Bennie and Gerry would travel together in his blue truck and Paul and I would travel in our hire car. Because we did this Paul and I had to wait until we reached Grandfather's home to hear of the amazing happenings on our way to see him. This is exactly as they recalled them to Paul and I before we met with Grandfather Martinez and his wife Grandmother Janice.

As red rocks came into view Gerry looked to her right and asked Bennie with a puzzled frown, "What lies over there in the vicinity of those red rocks?" Asking her why she replied, "Because I can see a huge funnel of energy over them. It looks just as it would if you were watching rain falling in the distance, with the lines of rainwater falling down to earth, but the lines are not rainwater they are pure energy falling downwards".

Bennie was fascinated but by now never questioned anything Gerry said for she had given him much proof of her psychic gift since meeting with her. "Where you are seeing the energy falling Gerry, that is directly over Grandfather Martinez land and home". He replied quietly.

"Oh!" was all she could say.

At last, we turned off the highway onto reservation land and almost immediately Gerry said, "There is a Warrior on a skewbald pony trotting in front of us. He is carrying a staff and wears two black feathers hanging down in his hair. It is Running Wolf. I wish you could see him". Alas we could not but Gerry kept up a running commentary for Bennie. Our journey continued for several minutes along the tarmac road with the Warrior trotting in front of the truck until we came to the end of the tarmac and a fork in the road to the right. Bennie hesitated momentarily then followed the right hand fork. Within seconds Gerry said, "Do you know the way then Bennie? Have you been here before?"

"Yes I have, I think this is the way".

"Are you sure?" she replied.

Turning to her he asked "Why?" Only to hear her say,

"It's just that Running Wolf has continued straight on and has halted. He has turned and is smiling at us. I'm sure he is waiting for us to follow him".

Without hesitation Bennie turned around and we continued to follow Running Wolf with Gerry in full flow. Having turned around we left tarmac behind and travelled along a dusty hard sun baked sandstone track. Now Gerry saw a medicine pouch being placed around Bennie's neck along with decorative beads and thongs. When she told him he said he knew what this meant. He told Paul and I later that as our journey progressed Gerry was almost unable to stay in the vehicle her excitement was so intense, for next she could see on every ledge and mountain top many Warriors Of Old appear on horseback. The horses were stationary, each one of them facing the direction we were driving and The Warriors Of Old, many of them in full ceremonial headdress, sat astride their mounts each holding a staff, and still Running Wolf trotted in front of our vehicles. All along the way Bennie waved continuously to each and every one of

The Warriors Of Old for although he could not see them he told her he could sense them. At the time Paul and I following behind could see him doing this but did not realise why. Meanwhile Gerry, bouncing around like a cat on a hot tin roof with excitement continued to describe all she could see.

Further along the track Bennie said, "There you are Gerry. Here is your coral and black snake you told me about in the list of clues you were given from the Spirit Warriors. Unfortunately it appeared so quickly from out of nowhere that we have run over it, but I have said a prayer for it. This was obviously another sign to show us we were heading in the right direction. Following this Gerry next saw a lone Eagle, and again was assured by The Warriors we were close to the person chosen to receive the gift of Spoken Truth.

Eventually we arrived at a wooden dwelling and immediately Running Wolf faded from Gerry's sight. Stiffly we climbed from our vehicles then Paul and I listened in astonishment as we were told of the amazing happenings, with Paul also being informed by his Mother that he was to represent us at the meeting with Grandfather Martinez. She had been told he had to do this by our Spirit Guide, The Watcher.

As the door was opened to us, Gerry and I could not fail to notice the verandah with the wooden chair along with the style of the building. In the book Spoken Truth she had described the dwelling exactly as we were now seeing it, along with Grandfather's chair where he likes to sit and meditate. Later on we would also have confirmation of the sacred spring on his land along with the single turquoise bead (mentioned in the clues given to us in the book). This turned out to be a single large rock, shaped like a turquoise bead and is extremely sacred to the Navajo people.

Grandmother Janice invited us into her home and Bennie introduced us explaining the reason for our visit at the same time giving Paul the opening to continue, whilst Grandmother Janice translated into Navajo for Grandfather Martinez. He can understand English a little but is more comfortable with his native tongue. The atmosphere was charged with suspicion, naturally so for Grandfather simply could not understand why the Elder we had met with on the previous evening had not deemed it necessary to be present to act as interpreter and mediator.

Feeling this long awaited meeting slipping away from us Gerry knew she had to step in and tried desperately, without causing offence, along with the help of Bennie to help Grandfather understand the sole reason we were there. Still the meeting did not progress well and Bennie was told by Grandmother Janice to leave the room and make a call to the Navajo Elder, telling him Grandfather needed him immediately.

With Bennie gone for a few minutes everything changed. Anxiety over this meeting had overcome Gerry causing her to lean on Bennie thus making her unable to listen to her Spirit Guides. Left on her own she had to calm herself and was able to receive guidance immediately from The Watcher. Gradually, with Grandmother Janice acting as interpreter, Grandfather visibly relaxed and as time passed he was able to understand we were there for one reason only – to hand over a Gift for his Nation. We wanted nothing in return. Receiving the following message for him from the Great Ancient Warriors we heard her say, "The Great Spirit honours you for your loyalty, commitment and passion to your Nation, the Navajo". On hearing this he wiped away silent tears as she handed him the copy of Spoken Truth produced on golden parchment like paper bound in gold ribbons with the beautiful psychic drawing of the white feather, unique to his copy on the inside cover. We were then able to show him the treasured pictures and watched intently as he felt these by vibrations (hence the trembling hands Gerry had seen). Amongst the many sketches and drawings is one titled 'Giver Of Dreams'. I was always certain this one portrayed the Keeper Of Old whoever he was, and when Grandfather Martinez saw it he was totally silent – for he too knew. He said one word. "Aho!"

He was very relaxed in our company by now and although we could see he was tiring as any person of his years would, his delightful sense of humour shone through. Following this Grandmother Janice fetched a small wicker basket and an extremely moving ceremony was performed, after which we were invited back to their home if ever we visited America again. Before we left, Grandfather Martinez said the book should be published in the Navajo tongue and asked Paul to carry the word forward to England and endeavour to have Spoken Truth published. Bennie was also given permission to use the book to spread the word across the Nations. Finally, after over three hours we left all feeling emotionally drained, totally unaware of what was to happen next as we made the return journey, and the following is Gerry's account of all she could see as we did so.

As we drew away from the dwelling and passed Grandfather Martinez's Hogan three Warriors appeared on horseback in front of Bennie's truck. They were The Watcher, The Chief and Running Wolf, all of whom were responsible for Spoken Truth. They trotted in front of us in full ceremonial clothing whilst at the same time all The Warriors previously positioned on top of the mountains and ledges were still astride their horses, only this time they were facing the way back and each horse was rearing to the sky with hooves continuously pawing the air, as if to salute us. Bennie was quite emotional and told us they were honouring us. This continued until we approached the long straight tarmac road. Here Gerry said she could hear hundreds of galloping hooves and suddenly The Warriors on the ledges etc., came down onto the road whilst being joined by hundreds more, all sitting astride their horses and ponies of all colours. They stood shoulder to shoulder on either side of the road as their mounts danced about on the spot pawing the ground continuously, and all the while we slowly drove on our way with the three Warriors trotting in front of us.

As we neared the end of the road Gerry was told to tell Bennie to stop for he had to pick up some of the dust from the road and throw it to the four corners of the world and all around him. He knew exactly why he was being told to do this telling her it was to honour Mother Earth and The Warriors because they had honoured us by showing themselves. Once he had done this he climbed back onto his truck and led us out of the gateway, whilst Gerry described how slowly the hundreds of Warriors turned away and started to leave.

As we travelled back to Grants, Gerry eventually calmed down enough to call her husband Tony from her mobile to let the families back home know we had completed our mission. He was thrilled then told her of the experience he had back home in England. At approximately the time of our handing over Spoken Truth to Grandfather Martinez, Tony had glanced up at the kitchen window of his home and saw a perfectly clear image of a White Buffalo on the glass. He could not believe what he was seeing. Not knowing what it meant he asked his daughter who did not know either, but on asking a friend to search on the internet they discovered it meant the completion of a prophecy.

With everything that had been happening to us since arriving in America we had not really been aware of the day and date, until I then realised it was the 18th August 2004. Exactly a year to the day that Gerry and I had started the journey which led to Spoken Truth being written and delivered to the Navajo Nation.

We had already been given the title of the second and third books before leaving for America which you are about to read, the contents of which have been entirely given by The Great Spirit who has made himself known to us now as **White Eagle**. We have also since been shown by **White Eagle** that the second and third books have to be joined as one. Book One – Nations Unite Within Souls We Walk. Book Two – Whispers Of Wisdom. Both of these come under the title Nations Unite Within Souls We Walk which as you will see **White Eagle** has offered to the Nations as his **Book Of Trust**.

* * * * * * * *

All you will read from this page onwards has been given from The Great Spirit White Eagle and many Warriors Of Old. No word or passage has been changed or altered by us. It is all solely as was given. The Spiritual drawings in the second part of this book Whispers Of Wisdom are not linked with the quotes and passages. They have been given to share with you.

* * * * * * * *

Geraldine Brolan and Lynda Shelton

1st October 2004

Each Warrior bring forth wisdom from souls inner doorways. Peace grows from souls of your world once we teach through Spoken Truth. Build together all followers once Spoken Truth reach many forms. New beginnings form rainbows to our Realm, walk within. Arcs of bright lights form, once doorways to own self open. Listen through heart. Sorrows dwindle once given doorways open within. All forms together bring harmony. Small droplets of Spoken Truth given from our Realm to your world. Believe words spoken change pathways of old, peace follows once words given from Warriors of time past. Each word spoken brings harmony once inner soul feels truth spoken. Look to no other form other than own self. Windows darkened by own sorrows. Trust own beliefs, know own truths. Teach. Learn. Gift of love shines bright amongst own world. Honesty, truth of own self will shine through to our window. We know many forms fall along pathways of own soul. Feelings deep within grow cold. Each fall we watch over. Eyes fear trust once fallen. Gift of love, light, honour, follows shadows. We walk beside all that fall upon your world. We feel sorrows deep within. Darkness falls beneath own footsteps. We gather all. We try to break free darkness from those who weep within. Time given to those few who we reach will break through walls of mistrust. We walk silently within all souls. We wait, we touch inner corridors of sorrow. Break free from own doorways of darkness. We give and shower bright lights. Take hold, give light to those who cross own pathways. Feel. Reach out arms of love to those who break own trust of own soul. Close no window to those fallen. Sorrows deep within close doorways to own beliefs. Shower all through own wisdom with gift of love, light and purity within. Tread slow. Footprints leave marks of time. Sands of time fall upon sorrows deep within. Mother Earth calls to those who bring forth pathways of whole new meanings. We bring all within brightness to guide along your own chosen pathways. Grow strong within. Help reunite all. Bring light upon golden sands. Trust. Move slow. Teach along the ways chosen. Learn all we give through heart. Gift of love we shower upon those who choose to bring light back to form many pathways of harmony.

2nd October 2004

Teach. Move within. Creator gold light. Close no door. Slow move mean footprints stay. Given those chosen forms words spoken from our Realm many moons past, we bring, we give whole new beginning within arms of followers. White woman chosen to break free old bonds of Nations troubled souls. Peace win. Shine bright past, now future shows ways forward through open doorways reached within souls. Peace grows. Teach form, white form Warrior, together unite Nations of your world. We try many followers to open hearts doors to begin roads of lightness. Pathways begin to shine once followers feel through own soul. Unite Nations. Trust own beliefs. Winters cold. Closed souls hard to break free. Ice forms mirrors of Mother Earth. Deep dark corridors hold many fears from within. Hold clear thoughts. Break bonds of fears driven beyond brightness. Shadow ones own inner fears. Cross over doorway to face shadows of darkness within. We channel our messages through souls of lightness. Peace follows footprints of our Realm. Gather knowledge. Tread slow. Feet firm. Bring forth writings to those chosen few. Pathways given to those chosen few. We shine through openness of own soul. Gather our thoughts together with own feelings. Cherish all we bring to honour all roots passed on from many forms. Truth given. Trust. Bonds of old give way to bright lights and peaceful thoughts once pathways chosen to honour Mother Earth. Nations fall. Peace broken through greed and mistrust of own hearts. Walk beside all forms around your world. Unite as one. Bring forth trust. Tread pathways. Link together all. Many hold deep sorrows within. We know sorrow. Leave behind darkness. Doorways begin to open once pain has gone. Brightness brings forth harmony. Trust. Believe your own thoughts. Clear window of own doubts. Share with those who believe in ways of lightness. We hear many sorrows pass over to our Realm from inner thoughts of own soul. Grieve only for those who die. Feel once grief understood. Listen voices from our open doorways. Many forms die young upon your world. Inside hearts, loneliness forms pockets within souls. Give love. Sorrow dwells only within corridors of darkness. Believe.

Those who leave own shell behind leave darkness within forever. Bright lights glisten to those who follow rainbows to our Realm. Heal those sorrows within. Broken trust falls heavy upon souls. Darkness covers many forms around your world. Peace given to those followers of our ways. Nourish those who believe. Trust truth spoken.

6th October 2004

We know sorrows deep within fear shadows walkways to own harmony. Never doubt those whose words teach all forms of wisdom. Rainbows form pockets of light. Windows to our Realm follow beyond archways of golden beams. All who learn bring back hope to Mother Earth. Nature follows footprints trodden many moons before you know as time. Knowledge grows within those chosen. Follow peace from within Brother to all Nations. Peace broken when Warriors die. All Nations speak of trust. Words spoken to many of peace, trust – fall. We try bring back hope to many Nations. Written words of truth spoken die within doorways. Windows cloud judgement. Many true words fall when inner souls troubled. Nations form groups. Each Warrior undertake own task within force. Nations close doorways to peace. Greed only brings sorrows of inner self. Nations break trust, bleed from wounds seep through Mother Earth's crust. Nation's followers speak only of war when troubled hearts. Sorrows deep within those who talk of peace. Nations fear those Warriors of darkness. Cold hearts within forms who rule. Each form born to lightness. Darkness within comes through time. Bright lights glisten from hearts of those who teach peace and trust. Within own soul take charge. Feel. Touch own soul before the essence of life fades. Place hand upon shoulder of friend. Teach harmony between Brothers. Follow footprints of own true being. We know pathways given hard to follow. Slow footsteps bring lightness of soul. Doorways on road lead to unknown places of inner self. Break free from those who form temptation of wrong doing to others. Teach heart to bring forth truth and trust. Once own soul free from bands of your ways touch others to bring forth new beginnings, pathways given to all when life begins. Many follow true beams of light. Many fall upon the pathway of darkness. We try to shine through all forms of Nations today.

8th October 2004

Each move brings forth roadways of time. Blame no other but each other. Words given, trust broken. Gather thoughts, prayers to each and all. Leave torment behind. Beings of your world gather forces under the flag of own beliefs. Nations emblems fly in the arms of Mother Nature's breeze. Trust gone from within of true and honourable ways. Wisdom of those within the pillar of trust blinkered from the vision of own inner soul. Teach only those followers of lightness to bring forces of darkness to an end. Peace follows all footprints of darkness, anger and torment once the gift of love enters within. Nations grow dark.

21st October 2004

Peace brings forth meanings of truth within darkest corners of Nation's wars. Each pathway chosen given to those followers of truths. Trust and belief brings forth brightness above all Nations sorrows. Clouds of judgement form corridors within souls. Beams of our trust, knowledge forms rainbows to all Nations. Pain dwindles from those suffering when bright light born within. True ways shown from high above once life begins. Roadways clear to all new beings. We watch over Nations life force. Souls walk pathways trodden long before time past, present. Now all future rests within arms of true followers of Mother Nature's harmony. Listen to hearts own feelings. Visions of the minds eye releases walls of darkness from within. We bring wisdom to those who realise true lightness of own soul. Teach all. Never doubt truth within. Trust own heart when given glimpses of our Realm through words spoken. Within many followers troubles follow. Wake the mind, release clouds. Wisdom brings forth bright lights. Each light begins footsteps to harmony of the soul. Never judge those who feel doubt of our words spoken. Learn to trust. Begin to walk the pathway of lightness. Reach out to those who follow in shadows. Never leave those who are troubled who fall upon the side of the road. Pathways bring those followers to our way of life. Bring lightness to dark shadows. Harmony will enhance all beings of true love. Peace follows slowly. Teach. Reach all those new beings born to your world. Within young minds visions will become reality once honour has been shown. Gift of lightness brings our words closer to troubled minds. Many followers who trust the word given from higher beings to show their way, speak of trust, honour and belief – bring shadows of doubt to own soul. Listen, take hold, search own heart to bring forth own truths. We live through forms who judge no one. We believe lightness will replenish the heart and soul of Mother Earth. Live through own beliefs. Search only for the love from others. Break free from own sorrows. Gather all. Mother Earth gives all, bears hardness to those who bring pain through earth's crust. Each wound heals. Mother Earth replenishes for all to live within the hope of harmony. Change the winds of darkness to bring forth new beginnings. Lights glisten once reached through arms of love. Prophecies go untold through many Nations of your world. Follow footsteps once trodden by those who believed. Rise above pathways of darkness. Feel strong. Strength given to those who try to bring forth inner peace. We know all. We keep watch.

27th October 2004

We know peace. Each troubled Nation brings upon each other disharmony within souls. Knowledge through arms of Mother Nature's wisdom shines through. Peace shall grow through strong minds of followers wisdom. Nations divide. Only fools fall upon pathways given. We ride winds of old through each corner of your world. Change own inner thoughts to pureness. Tread slow. Form pockets beneath own footprints. Never lead astray those innocents of mind. Darkness follows pureness. Once given in to shadows of darkness, weakness begins to grow strong. Strength of own self righteousness will begin to shine to our Realm. Giver of Spoken Truth brings harmony forward amongst many new believers once enlightened. Through followers of all Nations we know beliefs grow strong once Spoken Truth begins to move amongst people of your world. Many shine. Bright lights glisten through mists of uncertainty of many. Those who have no sight form visions of the soul to bring lightness within darkness. Those who see but cannot hear, feel through vibrations of all living and breathing creations. Know yourself. Bring forth own visions of need. Truths will grow only to those who follow pathways of lightness. We guide many followers. Justice will bring truth within own soul. Break honour and truths die from within. Give out love. Honour the hand given back. Once trust and honour has been accepted, follow wisdom of the heart, mind and soul. Peace follows only those who can accept the hand of those fallen upon the way of life. Courage of own self opens windows of the mind. Clear thoughts of pain, rise above the hurt that has been given within. Trust all we say. Victims of blindness trust hands of the soul. Within touch they build visions of the mind to know trust. Bring forth own doorways to feel through clouds of sight. Nations form blankets of darkness over all who breathe the air of Mother Nature's world. Time has no meaning to our Realm. Once walked upon your world, inner souls of our people know of honour and strong beliefs of the Creators way. We try to bring forth our wisdom to help the fulfilment of world peace as we know it now. Each footstep trodden on the pathway of lightness will stay, grow strong and imbed in Mother Nature's blanket around the core of life. Gift of laughter brings many tears of joy within soul. Sorrows dwindle when joy fills the heart. Innocence knows not of pain. Ways along life's pathway bring forth sorrows. Peace within the minds of the small child born to each woman and man will grow only if lightness within the heart of those given the gift of new life. Follow pathways of darkness, sorrows bleed to those innocent minds. Keep to the pathways of lightness, pain and sorrow will only touch but will never touch the inner soul of the gift of life through the love of each other.

28th October 2004

Each form bleeds from wounds done by others. Each wound heals. In time beliefs grown strong when lightness enters within souls open doorways. Reach the lightness from within. Close the doorways of darkness. Enter on to pathways of pureness. Each step trodden brings new beginnings to those who wander the pathways of the unknown. Each soul within fears not themselves but others. We try many ways to release those fears of shadows. Walk beside all. Doubt no others. Wish only lightness upon those who tread along broken pathways. We walk within many of your world. Teach only truth to one another before pain gathers coldness. Mother Nature hears sorrows when deeds of coldness are done to others. Change ways by giving lightness to those who break own rules of the soul. Judge no one but own self. Never turn from those who fear the golden rule of life. Live the way Mother Earth bestowed upon each and every one the true meaning of life, love and honour. This will bring back the true nature of peace to grow strong within all. Those who die upon the plains of your world fall upon the blanket of life which is shown to each and every one from our Realm. Gift of love shines brightly once Mother Nature wraps arms of lightness around those fallen. We know the ways of those who bring treachery and dishonour to those who walk the pathways of peace. Each soul whose light dies within we guide along the walkway of harmony and love. We embrace all that enter our Realm through the gateway of lightness. We give to those who wander through the mists of life. Trust and you will feel life's true meaning.

4th November 2004

4th November 2004

We bring Spoken Truth to form pockets of light, love and honesty within souls upon your world. Nature forms hope. Winged ones fly from your world above. Clouds are the blankets of Nature's force. Energies travel throughout rivers, mountains. Growth begins to flourish from within the heart of Mother Earth. Beams of light travel far beyond the circle that cradles your world. Wars within challenge the harmony bestowed within Mother Nature's core. Each troubled Nation creates distant tremors. Passageways to earth's core cease to close. Acknowledge the harmony given from long ago. We travel with many true believers who follow ways of old. Peace challenges discord. Many are troubled through fear. Nations of your world bring disharmony upon Mother Earth. Each form given a bright beam of light when born to the earth. Growth in many bears the edge of darkness. Forms differ in colour around your world. Each colour blinkers the true meaning of love. Life begins for all as one within. Nature carries birth for eternity. Fears take hold once small child grows. Teach the ways of trust. Take no corner shown. Bring all four corners to meet as one. Harmony follows through openness of the heart. Deliver peace to each one you touch through Spoken

Truth. Footprints of lightness follow once written words believed. Nations gather across the world. Many places form pockets of cruelty beneath the word religion. The good of God has no meaning to those followers of coldness. Many words for the one Creator have been chosen to guide each race along the pathway of known religions. Each way to many brings lightness to those followers who trust in the hearts of rulers. Within souls of high esteem the light dwindles. Greed and lust for power interferes in the true ways of the pathways to peace. Nations own rulers break trust of followers. Once given words of trust and truth from orders of high esteem, followers gather. Amongst many, trust and truth broken.

11th November 2004

Turn around, walk towards ones self, look within. Corners within souls harbour many forms of darkness. Inner fears shadow all forms of weakness. Anger shines from visions of sorrow. Many die through rage. Harbour angry thoughts within, wars begin to flourish. We meet souls from your world who die through beliefs of own people. Many follow footsteps trodden when Nations all around your world fight emblem of trust. Acknowledge the meaning of trust when forces begin the pathways of undoing towards Mother Earth's harmony of Nations. Begin to walk the line of trust when visions of own mind speak truths within own soul. Anger is the darkness you carry from within. Challenge the coldness of anger, listen to own heart and walk with me along the pathway of lightness to enable peace and harmony to flourish within. Nations rise against each other for the want of power to become powerful against each other. Many fall and die under the word of those in leadership. Thunder brings darkness from heavens above your world. We give lightness which flourishes from within. Each road passes by when thoughts are of ones self. Give arms of love when fears flourish. Cradle in the arms of Mother Nature when sorrow brings tears of pain. Laugh and bring lightness amongst shadows of sorrow. Many fool each other hiding behind falseness of true meaning of Nations' beliefs. Begin to follow the footsteps of time. Realize the whole meaning of lightness. Trust your judgement within own self. Truth brings forth new beginnings. Peace walks within from child who knows of no anger, rage or hate. Colour of skin bears no meaning to small child born within lightness and love. Many follow footprints trodden of own family sharing ways and beliefs. Those who trust the pathways shown by those who teach the way of life are blinkered by own needs. Listen. Take only what you know to be of lightness. Trust only in own heart. Never judge. Feel through own soul. Take hold and preach no words given.

17th December 2004

Forsake no one. Gift love, light shine within. Teach not preach. Walk as one with me. Blame no one. Together walk alone as the one true believer who carried the cross of burden for each and every one. Pathways shone beneath footprints trodden once long ago, given title from those who fear many forms who believe in love. Trust no other than yourselves true inner beliefs. Time as you want brings sorrows to all Nations. Lust, greed shines through shallow doorways. Poverty shares lightness through windows of love. Blame soars through valleys of darkness once trodden long ago. Each footprint trodden by lightness from man of true love bears no malice to those who walk the pathway of time. Together bring harmony back into those footprints trodden by the one true follower of love. Each pathway given to those believers. Mother Earth's goodness will leave marks upon the earth for which seeds will grow strong for all to share in the balance of Mother Nature's heart. Knowledge of past, present and future to come will change once followers of true love believe in all things of pureness within. Gateways open for all who wish to feel and touch the essence of love that shines in many who walk upon the pathways trodden many times before. We share worlds with others. Glimpses of our Realm are given to those see'rs to share amongst your world, in the hope of bringing lightness back upon the curtain of darkness that shrouds many who walk upon the carpet of Mother Earth's core. Gateways of darkness hide within each and every one.

Clear shadows from within. Let lightness seep to those dark corners. Love all and bring forth the balance of life as given when born.

27th January 2005

Many fall upon Mother Earth's carpet. Each step trodden lasts no longer than time itself. Place footprints under the wings of lightness. Beneath blanket of darkness many fall. We give lightness back through vibrations ringing through time. Zones known to our Realm go unnoticed upon your world. Each Warrior walk within the belief of truth. The balance of harmony rests within each and everyone. We guide followers to believe in lightness once within. Harmony follows through openness of own heart. Many carry burdens of mistrust. Spoken Truths dwindle from those doorways of darkness. Spread lightness, touch each other from within. Stand firm of own beliefs. Trust. Discard doubts of wants and needs. We give all. Those who trust feel our touch through own soul. Arms reach out to those fallen. Place hand upon shoulders. Teach. Unwillingness to learn brings forth corridors of loneliness. Each walkway given above all shines through the blankets of darkness once reached. Lust dwells amongst many. Bring truth to words spoken. Greed opens doorways of darkness. Lust gives pleasure to those fallen, leaves pockets of guilt beyond all feelings of love. Time itself known to your world has no meaning to our Realm.

4th February 2005

Each road grows in strength. Strong footprints left behind by those who walk beside me along the pathway of lightness. Readings trust. Time shows doorways, new beginnings flourish. Moons beneath our Realm give love, warmth when Spoken Truth begin. Many forms slow. Nations unite once given messages to all who wait. We know time meaning to us passes by without rushing. Smooth blankets cover rough ground once walked upon through words spoken. Each Warrior's place given. Trust. Hold fires of misbelief to within shadows. Piece together all Spoken Truth from our Realm. Listen. False truths rumble through time known to our Nation. Given doorways to your world open gateways once shown long before time as you know now. Messengers release prophecies together with trust, honour and truths spoken when each follower moved then upon Mother Earth's sweetest grasses. Gateways close to those forms whose footprints gather coldness. Each footprint given time changes once greed covers own true needs. Waters deepen through misuse. Thunder rumbles when darkness clouds judgement. Each pathway trodden within harmony, truth, brings lightness from those who believe. Mother Earth warns each and every one her needs, her wants and the hurts which harm the very nature of life itself. Messengers gather followers. Trust when given words from our Realm. Many misuse and destroy harmony. The balance of love gives way to anger. Guide the small to walk within lights of brightness. Heal those fallen upon the way. Feel through doorways to the heart of many troubled by own guilt. Touch those from within. Chains cold when given through darkness. Give out love through own beliefs. Move slow. Walk within the gateways of love, peace, truth and harmony. Shelter those who fear through loneliness.

9th February 2005

Indigenous tribes move within Mother Earth's bleeding heart. Treasure all, flourish within, blankets surround pathways shown to many followers. Listen to all those who believe in honesty of the soul. Nations Unite-windows form doorways to our Realm. We know being of the earth troubles dwell within. Give thoughts to those who practice no peace through doubts and self pity of own troubles. Lift the gateway to sorrow from within. Release darkness of doubt. Release fears of the unknown. Challenge own thoughts that cloud judgement of followers of the true meaning of peace. Many form trinkets of show when under the flag of truce. Nations own followers believe in all that is given from many who judge from within darkness of sorrow, misbelief. Judge only that of own soul not of those who break Mother Earth's carpet of lightness.

10th February 2005

Guide those who believe. Walk with me to pathways of glory. Mother Earth's core bleeds from sorrows of past and present. Change future. Start footsteps towards truths that lie between blankets of own greed. Nations follow shallow beliefs under the flags of own Nations. Trust when written words shown in all thoughts of peace, harmony and love. Lightness follows when shadows dwindle through trust and honour. Nations groan when deeds of hurt fall upon Mother Nature's carpet. Tread slow. Walk upon the blanket that is given with love from the source of life itself. Acknowledge own beliefs. Look within. Challenge own fears. Never doubt own thoughts, doubt those who ridicule. Freedom of the soul comes from within. Fears shut doors to our Realm. Believe me. REACH OUT FOR THE HAND OF LOVE I OFFER TO THOSE WHO CHOOSE THE RIGHT PATH OF ETERNITY. Nations of your world walked the line of truth. Each and every one take own pathways of life sheltering those close to the heart. Within each, teach the wrong from the brightness that we bestow upon new life. Many cause troubles when beliefs of own ways become memories. Troubled souls wander through life's pathway. Fears follow, troubles gain hold. Gateways given to all. Choose the pathways of trust. Honour brings back the force of nature itself. Emptiness fills with sorrow, breeds dishonour amongst many. Honour those who bring brightness back to those in number who wishes to walk free upon the sands of time. Many followers with guidance from our Realm walk the pathways given to share our teachings spoken from many in the hope of your world becoming a bright star once again. Follow guidelines written in words and from the hearts of all that share the footsteps walked by many through time known as years by your world. Given trust to the chosen few who walk upon the sands of peace. Each step trodden by those who wish to follow in the lightness will bring harmony to own heart. Shadows walk within anger. Fears cause troubled souls to wander through darkness. Reach those who pass through your gateway. Offer the hand of love to those. Each step will guide those to within the circle of light. Nations trust dwindles from afar, peace moves slow. We reach many through 'Spoken Truth' once believed. Pathways given to those of your world, each pathway chosen in life have meanings to all. Judge no one who chooses the wrong pathway. Guide along the way in hope of bringing lightness back to those who fall within darkness. Teach only from the heart. Trust through the soul, gateways open.

11th February 2005

We bring 'Spoken Truth' to within your world to reach all beliefs through love. Preach no words given. Speak to those followers the words of our teachings. We give lightness. Thoughts of peace come from souls of many who crossed the pathway of brightness to our Realm. Sadness flourishes from doubts through sorrows, grief and discord. Many dwell upon the passing of those close to the heart. We reach through time zones to shelter and bring all to within the true meaning of lightness. Peace follows the walkway to our Realm. Guides allow all to cross over the darkness before lightness to meet loved ones from time past. People teach the meaning of love. Listen to the words spoken. Feel through soul. Take each word within. Nations hold dear words given to those who teach under the emblems of own beliefs. Ways shown bring about wars not peace and harmony. Listen to those who teach ways of own beliefs. Listen. Learn. Trust only in soul. Windows close to those who bear anger to all to ways not of own. Many glimpse our thoughts through visions of the mind. Hear words spoken through mind. Followers trust when glimpses of our Realm given. Each footstep taken on the pathway of righteousness close doors of darkness. Search within to follow your pathway given when life itself began. Within your world many die young, old, taken from Mother Earth's carpet, each soul taken from the shell given to each and everyone. We take charge when many walk the bridge to our Realm. Each soul reaches our Realm through windows of pureness. We teach to all who passes through our gateway. Those who falter from life itself walk upon the roadway leading to own sorrows. Gifts 'Spoken Truth, Nations Unite Within Souls We Walk', given to your world in the hope of reaching those who wish to walk in peace upon the pathway to our Realm. We speak to those who walk the roadway back in the hope of bringing inner peace. Many redeem own sorrows, challenge own guilt's of time past, bringing lightness to within. Bright lights glisten, shines upon the pathway to enable those to walk upon the bridge to our Realm.

23rd February 2005

Challenge darkness from within. Own doorways glisten when truth replenishes own fears. Each walkway upon your world brings forth openings. Trust each pathway walked upon. Beginnings unfold from within when trust, honour and beliefs shine through. Windows open to your Realm when honour bestowed upon own beliefs. Each child wanders from within. Corners unfold. New beginnings shine through once peace flows through body's own rivers. Nations unite. Forces of darkness dwindle once beliefs, true beliefs, shine through army's forcefulness. We cherish all beliefs beyond our source. Lights shine through. Cherish all from within native to your own true worth. Winds change forms of time. Seas regain land stolen from Earth's core. Beliefs dwindle from hearts of many. Sorrows grow strong from within. Child knows of no such sorrow from life force itself. Teach only truth. Trust. Many follow darkness. Walls harden from within. Take charge. Bring forth bright lights. Shelter no darkness. Forces dwindle through beliefs. Many Nations gather within the circle of lights. Enter through doorways given. Open up windows to our Realm. Walk with me through times of sorrow. Bring all beliefs from within. Show true love to those fallen upon troubled pathways. We share all our wisdom to those followers who believe in our Realm. Gather thoughts with each follower. Nations grow strong within pockets of brightness. Each follower give to those who bring fears of own heart to within the bright lights of those who believe in our Realm. Share wisdom, knowledge, to those who believe in our word, spoken to those who reach our Realm. Acknowledge all troubled. Bring hope to within those who ride the waves of troubled waters. Each follower entrusted to walk upon the pathway of pure light. Forbidden grounds ride strong through your world. Each Warrior then, now break the forces of darkness from within. Spread lightness upon the grounds of Mother Earth. Harmony follows blankets of darkness. Believe. Open all. Gaze upon the darkness from within. Shed those fears. Hold only pure lightness and peace will follow. Each pain reaches our Realm. We gather thoughts from all.

25th February 2005

Nature's force changes many marks around your world, leaves many pockets of destruction throughout. Visions given to those see'rs upon the pathway of life. Warmth gathers shards of light from within. Each carries forth particles to within the walkways chosen to enhance the love within. Many challenge beliefs of Nations around your world. We shine through many teachings to bring the balance of all back to within the unity of Mother Earth. Nations follow within circles of force. Choose only the right from the wrong. Give to those who follow the pathways of unity between the life force of all and the being of Mother Earth's core. We know peace from within. Lights burn bright once the heart opens to walk the pathways of peace and harmony. Allow those to touch and unite true feelings of the soul. Nurture own beliefs to allow many to reach the doorways open for all to meet the one true to man. Many walk with me through life's corridors. Understandings of works moving within the force of our Realm will enhance all to those who cherish the meaning of love, which we cherish within hearts of many.

4th March 2005

Walk with me along the pathways trodden by man long ago. Place heart upon the stone of life which burns within each and everyone walking upon Mother Earth. Sayings bring forth words written from Warriors of time passed. Within, much can be told to followers who believe in life carried on from within the shell given to all as life began for each soul. Honour bestowed upon all who carry forth meaning of lightness itself. Open heart for which the light of life burns within. Harbour mistrust within shadows walk. Doubt follows when mistrust enters through the doorway of life. Many follow through own want. Listen to those who try to teach ways of truth, honesty given back once doorways open to ways of changing Mother Earth. The candle of light burns bright from within those who walk upon your world. Each flame carries forth the essence of what lies beneath the true self. Within those who falter upon the pathways given to follow, rays begin to dwindle. We try to bring back the spark to each flame that is darkened through deeds done by many. Many walk upon the land taken from true believers of old. Beneath Mother Earth's crust life burns from the core of your world. Mother Earth gives back sorrows from deep within. Each pocket channels energies of burning embers that flow. Within each force, life falls beneath. Embers grow cold when winds of change channel their energies to the hurts of Mother Earth. Life begins to form upon each blanket that covers the crust of Mother Earth. Each Warrior gives lightness to true followers who believe in the ways of Mother Earth. Sorrows lay beneath the carpet done by many through time itself. Hurts bestowed upon Mother Earth gathers darkness from within. Each follower chooses lightness to carry forth the words given to heal the wounds that linger through time. Once belief strong to many who walk upon Mother Earth, changes begin to flourish from deep within. Seeds grow strong. Rivers flow within replenishing all. We gather seeds of hope from each follower. Travel with me along the pathway of love. Lightness will follow from those strong believers. Many Nations fear those who teach from our Realm.

6th March 2005

Transform thoughts of worth and walk with me. Beseech those who fall. Earth tremors bring forth emptiness for which Mother Earth's heart bleeds from within. All within pathways near to those faults that open, crumbles to dust. Nations forces bring to light ways for which burdens are left to those few who remain the force to which all believe. Guidance from those who fly emblems of their own trust gather all within pockets of truth. Many who walk with me gaze upon the true love from others who gather amongst each Nation. Faith follows own true beliefs. Walk hand in hand with those who follow the true being as one. Blame no one. Leave doubt for those who trust in own self pity. Time wanders through zones that cannot be seen. Each being carries forth harmonies of each Realm. Your world our Realm, meet within zones known only to souls who walk the bridge to eternity. We give love to those who cherish all beings given from the one Creator. Each walk beside each other, hands held high to those followers who bring life force back to within the true ways given to embrace Nature's life force. Embrace all who cross within the pathway chosen by each who follow the pathway touched by the essence of truth. Man brings forth shadows around your world seeping through the channels of life. Clouds form once inner lights fail to shine brightly. Take hold of own inner fears. Change thoughts of emptiness into thoughts of pureness.

11th March 2005

People shine through all Nations of the world. Challenges are put before each and every one. The given ways shown are of peace and harmony. Choose the pathway given to enhance life itself. Choose other pathways, choices are taken from within sight. Many choose the wrong path. Given one becomes reality to those true believers. Each path trodden within the footsteps of life challenges own beliefs. Nations begin to follow others along the routes of darkness. Wars blanket Mother Earth's softness. Nations trust own words of reality. Within reality to those who dwell upon the wrong pathway hope dwindles through mistrust, dishonour and greed. Pathways known to followers of righteousness walk within harmony. Glimmers of hope spread wide amongst Nations to which brightness follows pathways beneath the flag of truce. Within each step trodden lies beneath glimmers of lightness. Mother Earth cradles footsteps of truth. Hearts grow strong once belief grows within. Trust those who bring truth to within each footstep trodden. Place hand upon the arm of those followers. Lead. Begin to trust in own self. Each hand moves amongst those followers. Doubt dwindles once touched through the window of the soul. We give to those who believe trust, honour and peace. Forgiveness is given to those who walk within the line between lightness and darkness. Once trust is acknowledged pathways open to within the bright lights of love. Place all knowledge of life together with the belief of truth and harmony. Walk with Mother Nature's breezes, shine for eternity.

13th March 2005

Place trust in those few who walk the line of life. Within each who follow own code of honour will enhance the meanings of beliefs through many who falter within own righteousness. We bring to those who believe words of wisdom to follow through the pathways of life itself. We bring words of wisdom to each who wish to join with me the pathway to enable life's cycle to continue amongst people who walk upon Mother Nature's softness. Share with one given truth from within. Each one touched by only one meaning will enable all to flourish by spreading arms of purity within. Teach all meanings of the heart to those who bring joy to within the home of love. Born to each, joy will enhance for ever more. Once given, true honours passed from the heart to within each, will enable those to follow own codes written from within the hearts of true beings, of the meaning of love, given by me with the hope of all Nations to come to follow the pathways of lightness trodden by many followers of the one which carried all within, to enable richness to flow amongst races around your world for as long as life itself burns like the candles which are bestowed within each and everyone born to man.

Wandering dew forms pockets within pockets. Cascades of morning dew gathers momentum for which rivers drink. Centuries go by for which we know of sorrows. Gather all teachings, our wishes to fulfil roadways of darkness when teach meanings. Kaleidoscope of brightness glistens through our rainbows of hope. Treasure each blessing given to fulfilment of courage. Hold no judgement for which pain, sorrows flow through the soils of Mother Earth. Each window opens doorways to teach through 'Spoken Truth, Nations Unite' and forthcoming teachings, warmth given to within all troubled hearts through the unjust of reason. Movement within each office of belief brings forth many sorrows. Remember we know, we hear and we touch those troubled through the darkness that is closed when life itself taken. Blame troubles the heart, carries pockets within the soul of injustice. Nations bring barriers of harm to within all walkways of life. Man falls before coldness once driven beyond the glimmer of trust. Waste no force of energy and mistrust no other than each other. Pathways given to those who understand life itself, wisdom falls within once greed gathers footsteps trodden by own self esteem. Nations followers of purity gather forces of pureness within the folds of lightness entrusted to those beliefs given to enhance the forces of Mother Nature. Wish not for own self, wish for those who bring the balance of true life beneath the Wisdom Keepers of time past. Each Warrior given tasks to undertake in the true meaning of harmony, which in turn brings forth true balance of all that walk upon the carpet of love given by the heart and soul risen from the source of pureness herself. Time risen for all to share many beliefs. Walk with me through shadows of darkness. Each corner reached within, forces the light to bring forth openings in the hope of all to share in the gentleness which surrounds the Nation of which you belong. Man's troubled hearts carries the force of darkness to those who walk the pathways of purity. Rivers of hardness within those troubled will enhance the realm of darkness. Seeds scattered amongst many grow through own strength of truth. Peace of many flows within the troubled soils spread across the flesh of Mother Nature. Wisdoms forces enter through cracks given by the life entrusted to each and everyone who wishes to enhance the flow of energies given by Mother Nature's heartbeat.

18th July 2005

Place trust beneath windows openness. Nations walk tall beneath weaknesses. Guidance to walk within the corridors of loneliness. Between light and dark rests the pathway given to choose own destiny, given choice to bring peace amongst many who walk within the bright lights entrusted to each from the beginning of time itself. We give wisdom to share before all. Manifest the light once more to bring forth harmony which glimmers for eternity within own form. Shadows follow beside each and everyone. Trust own heart. Bring forth pureness from within to spread the blanket of love amongst those who cross beneath own footsteps. Never doubt the love shared by many who wish to continue and enhance the powerful meaning of truth, honesty and the power of love given to share amongst all. Nations blinkered to the words given from our Realm. Walk tall amongst the ones chosen to share the teachings. Acknowledgement of those who follow beneath the words spoken by all in High Order, given under the flag of trust. Begin to search within the true meanings of the words given. Search own soul to bring forth true meanings of those whose guidance shows openness from within. Doubt those who bring forth messages of war. Beneath the tears of harm doorways of darkness will follow. We know we share amongst your world the sorrows of many. Leave no shadows of pain within. Release the harm, the hurt done by those who bring forth widespread pain. Blankets of lightness shroud those fallen under the guidance of those who bring forth burdens of misunderstanding. We give those who choose the pathways of lightness to bring forth the meanings of purity amongst races around Mother Nature's heart, the openness, the wisdom to follow and to share amongst the ones who choose to walk along the pathways covered in the rays of our love. Within the openness of purity, understandings grow from the soul of each who walk beside the true meaning of love. Disharmony causes many feelings of doubt amongst which darkness forms pockets around own self. Clear those doubts from within. Start to rekindle the warmth to which nurture and feed the energies that surround all living things. Nature's arms feel through the warmth given from within. Sorrows dwindle once the lights shine brightly. Colourful beams glisten from each who wish to walk the rainbow path of love and the true meaning of harmony. These lights that glisten from each who choose to bring forth peace and harmony link together and form archways of pureness. Feed only from the heart and soul of those who bring forth the love and the lightness. Bring forth openness to walk amongst each race. Share the love given from the one we all know and understand to within the beliefs you've chosen to follow. Give back understandings to each born within the sanctity of the heart. Nations begin the growth of humanity. Peace follows once each belief understands the true meanings and shares amongst those followers who walk beneath the emblem of truth. Shelter no man from within. Guide along the pathways trodden from when man first walked upon Mother Earth's carpet. Guidance brings forth trust. Trust brings forth the true meaning of peace within each soul who walks within the lightness given from those fallen, past, present and for those to fall within the time to come. Amongst these each redeem own sorrows before the bright lights that shine the pathway for all eternity.

26th July 2005

Future forms mirrors of your world long before. Each sparkle of iridescencey forms droplets within. Guidance within grows strong.

From the centre of each sparklet transforms energies to which enhances the waters that surround all creations upon Mother Earth's carpet. Droplets of pureness soak within the roots that form beneath soils. Nourishment from each life force beneath Mother Earth will give the pureness within to nourish the vein of life which each and everyone feeds the soul of own self. Cover the pathway of trust, honour and belief with the arms of those which walk beside each and everyone. Give to those who wander, the honour to which races of all creeds belong. Covenants broken when acts of harm done to each living, breathing energy. Turn own beliefs to which the growth of self esteem will flourish, to begin the balance of harmony, to enable all to start the walkway to bring Mother Earth's forces to within the bright lights that surround the world of today. Given own choice, choose wisely and enhance the breath of life to which seeds of the future will grow tall amongst the Nations. Weak seeds wilt and fall beneath the crust of Mother Earth. These seeds will feed and nourish the birth of all creations to enable the flow of the stream of life to walk free once more upon the soils given by love. Many who choose from within their heart and soul, will choose to believe in the lightness that surrounds all Mother Nature's creations. The meaning of the words spoken from each Warrior of time past, will enable all to help lift the blankets of darkness that walks beside each who fall upon the way of life itself. Shower just a few thoughts of pureness from within own self, energies for which will feed and nourish all who wish to walk beside those chosen to feed the energies given for all to share amongst

Nations of the world today. Life begins from seeds sown by many. Bring forth rainbows of harmony once life is born to man. Each child will then grow amongst the peace and harmony of those who nurture within the bright lights entrusted from the one true being born to man. Share amongst all who walk within the circle of hope. True meanings of the words spoken by many, given in the hope of all who walk upon Mother Earth to enable all who bring forth messages of love, truth and honesty which gathers all energies within the words given of peace and harmony. Balancing Nature's energy sources will enable the life cycle to begin the pathway to which life itself gathers the iridescence of pureness.

29th July 2005

Water sources flow beneath the crusts and soils that cover the soul within Mother Earth's core. Nourish the waters that rise above. Each trickle brings forth nourishment to share the blood given from the rains absorbed through the carpet of life given from the energies within the core of the world today. Place beneath own footsteps the joys that are to be shared amongst all Nations who spread arms of love across the plains of existence. Many forces bring death amongst all races to which the pain from the sorrows gathered within each and everyone, causes Mother Nature's energies to absorb the hurts that flow beneath the footsteps trodden by each and all. Within the footsteps trodden, the energy source flows deep within the crevices and cracks opened by the pains that dwell beneath the crust given to protect the life source of Mother Nature's energies. Weaknesses within the life force of many begin to cause the burdens and the harm before which everyone has to carry upon themselves. Share amongst those who fall from the pathways shown by ancient forces, the ways given to bring the energies of pureness back to within the reach of those who wish to follow the pathways given to enhance the harmony of Mother Nature's breath. Lightness follows the shadows given by those who break the balance of the wondrous gift of Mother Nature's whispers. Each whisper that is heard amongst the winds that carries the energies that flow within the ring of the life force shared by all. Balance within own self will radiate through the energies that surround each and everyone. Vibrations seep through the lands that are walked upon by every man, woman born to within the circle of life. The forces from which Mother Nature feeds upon, repairs damages done by many. Each time the winds carry the pains done to Mother Earth to our Realm, we gather together in the hope of reaching those chosen to bring forth the love and the harmony given by many to enhance the rays that shine through and bring forth Nature's balance.

8th **August 2005**

Place soul beneath wings of dove. Walk beside all who follow righteousness. Guidance, choices, given to many who wish to walk tall for all eternity. Place trust amongst only those who bring forth the wings of peace. Spread those wings amongst those who cross over the pathway chosen by each who walk beside the emblem of truth. Trust only fears from the heart. Seek no revelance. Bring justice to within own soul. Reach forward amongst the love given by those who wish freedom for each and everyone. We give rays of love carried on the winds given by Mother Nature for which envelops the clouds that surround those who have doubts. Each born to man, pathways given. Choose wisely. Bring forth the new beginning and enhance the love shared by those who bring teachings of peace and purity amongst those who share the rays of hope. Born within the love of each, carry forth, nurture and bring forward the love entrusted on each born. Carry this love amongst those. Share troubles, pain enhanced by grief. Cover those who bleed from within with the arms of love. Treasure the moments shared, for the pathway of love begins from within own self. Touch many. Each brush of the hand leaves imprints within the soul. Few words absorbed by teachings given by our world will grow in time. Break the chains of hurt, start the circle of lightness within own self. Radiate from within the love. Share amongst those who wish to walk free the joy of Mother Nature's surroundings. Peace together the broken pieces of time and reunite the harmony once more.

11ᵗʰ August 2005

Reach forth, take hold. The breath of Mother Nature enlightens within each and all. Nourishment feeds from within. Many falter beyond the gateways entrusted upon each when given the breath of life. Each step trodden releases energies, to which the core of Mother Earth stores within the crevices enhanced by the deeds done by man. Each walkway entrusted upon those chosen to release the pain absorbed within the veins that flow within the circle of life. Beneath the shell of humanity, flows the essences of purity. Within each and all, break free the wondrous gift of love and life itself to change the ways trodden by those who walked upon the carpets laid down around the nakedness and purity, and bring truthfulness within peace and harmony. Give love to those who wish to follow the lightness that surrounds true believers in the ways forgotten by many. Gifts given under many beliefs ring bells of openness to which energies sing on the wings carried by the breezes shared amongst all. Messengers ring bells of trust from which meanings of our teachings penetrate deep within the heart and soul of those who wish to carry forth the true meaning of our words spoken within the harmony of Mother Nature's presence. Guide those who wish to tread amongst the imprints left by those who teach within the words spoken. Those who wish to follow for eternity will bring forth new beams of joy. These reach far beyond the energies that surround the world of today. Echoes of past torments dwindle when touched by the essence of joy.

'Spoken Truth' gives the journey of time past. Within each word spoken releases vibrations to which hope carries on Mother Nature's breeze. Each pathway chosen by those who wish to bring the true meanings of peace and harmony to within the four corners of the world today, will help to release the energies buried deep within the heart and soul of Mother Nature. Vanquish all doubts from within. Openness releases pureness of the soul. Bring forth own doorway to walk upon the golden pathway of life. Begin to nourish from within and enjoy all gifts of Nature's openness.

16th August 2005

Peace walks tall amongst many Nations. All who wish to begin on the road to enhance the true meaning of the word given in our teachings, will ensure the fruitfulness to flourish amongst all races around the world of today. Bring forth own beliefs of purity to enable all to flourish within family circle. Each barrier lift. Each crossroad choose wisely. Doubts amongst those fears will diminish once looked upon from within. Many crossroads bears negative movements of which gather together the true meanings of which own doubts cause Nature's own disasters. When given the choice to walk upon stony ground or softness of the sands given by Nature's own purity, choose to walk beside those who wish all to flourish within the harmony to bring forth the balance of time past. Future exists within each and everyone who walks upon the blankets laid down by Mother Nature. Wisdom comes from beliefs of those with true teachings. Those who wish to walk within the harmony given by those followers who reach amongst all Nations of today's world, will enable the lightness to shine through, and show the way to those who carry the balance of peace and harmony back to within the hands of all who wish to join the pathways trodden by those of time past. Break free from the angers, the sorrows and the pain that all harbour within. Once released and all understood, will open doorways and start the new understanding of the words chosen to enhance the true meanings of all who walk within the rainbow of lightness. Each word given in the hope of understandings to which all new life should be given the true pathway to walk upon. The words spoken are of peace, truthfulness, harmony, love and purity. These should be carried amongst the races of today who bring upon each and everyone misunderstandings of life itself. Needless hurts leaves blemishes upon each. Never do wrong to those who have wronged. Leave lightness to within the pain which forces darkness to dwindle. Once the hurts have diminished, lightness seeps through. Within this lightness the heart and soul will rekindle the love forgotten by many. Shower each who cross over pathways laid down within the love given by those who suffered the agonies of war of time past and present and those who will suffer in time to come. Share much from within. Each thought radiates pureness. Each thought carried far beyond to those whose fears harbour judgement of themselves. Wake those forgotten beliefs from deep within. Nurture own self along the roadway forgotten under the emblem of trust. To reach deep within and understand the meanings forgotten, will bring pureness to within the lightness given by life. Waste not meaningless thoughts of self pity. Tread slow amongst the fears of own self. Place trust amongst all. Break free from chains of coldness. Open the doorway of the heart that beats within. Turn around and look upon the footsteps that each and everyone leaves behind in the sands of time. Take each footstep trodden and search within and undo the pain given to those who have wronged own self. Never judge amongst those wrong doers. Each have been given the choice to undertake the truth. Each pathway chosen to walk upon will bring forth many obstacles to cross. Balance together the life and the love and choose to walk the pathways of honesty, which in time will turn all walkways back to within the bright lights that shine and radiate from deep within each and everyone who wish to walk within peace and harmony of Mother Nature's arms of purity.

18th August 2005

Walk within the righteousness of own truths. Begin to shower all who cross own path with the light and love we share from the birth of time itself. Never show judgement within the trust given. Allow knowledge of own self to be shared amongst all who walk many pathways. Within the shadows of mistrust place the seeds of wisdom to allow the growth of each and all to flourish within the circle of life itself. Meanings of many truths change from Nation to Nation. All follow the true ways of trust and honesty. Give lightness to enable the love to flourish amongst many who fall along the pathways of life. Begin to envelop the true meanings of worth. Give to those who wish to follow the right pathways to within the circle of hope, the true beliefs and understandings of the ways given. Begin to understand the meanings of own beliefs from within. Teach only the truth. Never doubt amongst those who share own true feelings. Give time to understand each Spoken Truth from those who walk beside each and everyone. Place arms of softness around the ones who doubt own beliefs. Feel through the window of the soul to enable the understanding to which words spoken can bring forth and nurture and enhance the true way of life. Many people who listen amongst those who preach the words given from time past, misunderstandings of the words spoken many times fall within the shadows of mistrust. Time heals sorrows deep within. Nurture and cradle those who suffer through pain done by many. Give back the trust broken from within the source from the words used under the meaning of trust. Once trust is cradled within those, begin the pathway of truth. Lead not force. Given abundance of true lightness to within each. Allow the mistakes made by those who walk amongst many races to teach the true meanings of which many fail to understand. Each pocket of sorrow reaches deep within those true followers. Many wish to force upon each and all there own strong beliefs. To undertake all truth of those who preach under many emblems, confuse and cause the mind to be troubled. Seek own beliefs amongst own feelings. Piece together the issues laid down by those in high authorities. Reach forward and only take the words that are understood by own self. Each pathway trodden and each gateway opened will enhance the meanings of life amongst those who wish to gain the knowledge and understandings of many Nations. Leave behind the doubts and look to within the bright lights given for all to share.

22nd August 2005

Begin to flourish through words of wisdom. Many pathways clear once belief feeds through the flow that washes through each and every one. Pathways clear from the burdens collected along the way of life. Understandings begin to flow once sorrows and pain understood. Nurture those within the home. Give understandings and teach along the way. Bring forth own true beliefs of how and why. The understandings given justify all truths spoken within each family's own circle. Ways begin to open for those who ride the waves of hope for all in the justification of the worth in balancing the nature that surrounds each Nation around the world of today. Once meanings understood, pave your own footpath with the beams and rays of the sunshine of hope. Performing small deeds of love and lightness will enhance the vibrations to within the ambiance given off by Mother Nature's heartbeat. Waste not the waters given by the rains that fall from the clouds of storms. Each raindrop given to feed the seeds that are sown through time itself. Redeem those shadows that dwell within each and everyone. Change the lifestyle to within the balance of own worth. Give plenty, take little of what is needed. Style depicts nothing. Honour depicts plenty of worth. Carry forth the true meanings of the word of love within the home. Reach the balance of love within the home by giving the understandings for which all will grow strong once the true meanings for each are reached and understood. Many falter upon the pathways of life. Fear travels within each and everyone. Food feeds the body, harmony balances the soul. Teach the meanings of truthfulness to those who begin the pathways of life. Each child remembers happy thoughts. Pain stays deep within. Give comfort to the pains done by those along the pathways of life. Tread slow when teaching those the ways of life within the family home. Break no promises given. Balance comes from within own circle of life. Give trust and trust will be given. Give the understandings to those who falter within your own beliefs. Many who wish to climb the peaks of greed pave their own destiny. Take all, give nothing, enhances nothing. Take little, give plenty, enhances the life cycle of each enabling the world of today to walk within the life cycle of hope. Many words written in many forms will reach those true believers who walk the pathways of righteousness. Harmony comes in many forms. Take upon yourself the one that teaches you the wisdom and the ways of love. Balance own self through the way chosen. Words spoken will teach those who wish to speak only. Words given in the ways of song will be remembered by many and will continue to ring the bells of harmony. Each way chosen will bring forth the teachings and the true ways believed within each.

26th August 2005

Preach no ways to others. Take the hand of all who walk within your own pathway. Guide along the way. Teach those wisdom and truthfulness and walk beside. Bring forth, nurture. Place before all the lightness from within to enhance all in abundance with the true meaning of life. Balance comes to all those who wish to bring fulfilment within the heart of Mother Nature's energies. Truthfulness radiates throughout those who reach forth and bring the true balance within Nature's own walkways. Give love and lightness to all creatures that walk upon the carpets that surround the world of today. Nature balances out all creations through walkways of life itself. Seeds fall from within the arms of Mother Nature's breezes. These carried upon the winds of time fall upon the carpets to which new life begins for all to feel, see and nourish from. Those who wish plenty gain nothing. Those who wish nothing reap plentiful for all to share amongst true believers of Mother Nature's harmony. Look within all teachings from within. Gain the knowledge and wisdom we share amongst all. Reap only what is needed to follow the true wisdom and ways of the one Creator of all creations. Nestle within the heart and soul of each and everyone the love and lightness we share to enable the way of life to begin upon the pathway laid down by many of time past. Footsteps trodden within the true way of life shine strong within the rays of hope given to all in the hope that many will bring back the true balance within the life given to all Sisters and Brothers around the world of today.

29th August 2005

Many fear those who believe in the teachings laid down by those who walked upon the earth of time past. Within all given, take upon oneself the wisdom and true meanings of each passage given by many. Free doubts and fears will dwindle. Share amongst those who walk beside you. Give meanings of own beliefs to those who need explanations of the words spoken. Many choose to express own feelings in ways to share and express emotions that dwell within. Words spoken in song share feelings of sorrows, joy. Words given in rhyme join together emotions that dwell deep within. The hand releases energies to which forms visions from within the minds eye. Within each chosen, many collect and keep within the home. Release and nurture in abundance the true meanings of all given. Science releases doubts for which unexplained amongst many. Search within and teach own self the explanations and understandings and walk beside those who believe in the energies given off by all creations. Explain no meanings of life to which all born hold the energies within. Each man, woman and child walk freely upon the pathways given in life. Mother Nature feeds each and everyone. Energies give life to all. Science accepts these energies for which we all feed upon. When each life force dwindles and the candles within cease to glow, energies from within the shell releases through the doorway of the soul. Believe in life beyond life as you know it and share in the world beyond.

31st August 2005

Nature's treasures give life to all who live amongst the winds of time. Give peace to those who share the beauty of all that surrounds each living energy. Turn all thoughts and vibrations to walk within the bright lights that glow within. Share amongst those who wish to join in the struggle to bring the peace and harmony back to Mother Nature's arms. Gentleness flows within the veins of each born to man. Gifts given to those chosen from within the true meaning of peace and harmony. Gather together, move amongst and share all knowledge and wisdom given by many of time past. Words spoken under the true meaning of truth will enhance the true being of ones self. Shine from within and balance own energies which radiate amongst the Nations all around the world. Peace will begin to move slow amongst the footsteps marked down by the chosen Warriors who walk beside each and all. Remember the footsteps trodden from time past. Bring back the glory to within own self. Radiate love. Gifts given share amongst those who have little. Shine amongst those who believe and trust in all creations. Never doubt the wisdom and the truth spoken by those Warriors who walk the pathway to enhance peace and harmony and who share in the struggle of bringing purity back to within the arms of Mother Nature. Strangers who cross own footpaths, reach for the hand and offer nourishment through words spoken in the lightness of the wisdom shared by those true believers of Nature's truth. Fear not the openness of each doorway to our Realm. Gather together and unite with those who share in beliefs. Each belief will walk beneath own emblems. Never judge but share same beliefs with all those and change the destinies of destruction. Rekindle through lightness and love and bring the balance of all energies that radiate from all living things, to enable each and everyone to start the journey forward and change the hurt and the pain that dwells amongst so many who wander along the roadways laid down upon the carpets that surround the world of today.

1st September 2005

Place beneath each walkway of life the love and understanding to teach the purity of life itself. Never take upon own self judgement of those who walk amongst the shadows of wrong doing. Allow the understanding to teach all with guidance the true meanings of the words spoken to enable all to flourish within. Time itself allows the sorrows we share amongst each to bear the burdens of troubled times to walk beside all. Lift the hurt and pain from within, release the energies of lightness. Bear no grudges, take upon oneself the understanding of world peace and join together. Unite with all and share together. Reach the golden glory of peace. Bring the harmony back to within the walkway of Nature's serenity. Troubled waters shift amongst Nations. These bring forth the destruction of much. Waves force energies upon the lands. Within the manifestation of the waters life begins to unite together. Walk amongst and share in the pain and grief of those whose light dwindles from within. Support and teach each other. Nurture those whose life begins from within troubled times. Each life born to man releases energies of pureness. The gift of love share within the home. Teach wisdom of peace and bring forth the balance of life. Walk amongst those who share in the hope of bringing harmony back to all Nations around the world of today.

14th October 2005

Waves of energy flows through Mother Earth's core. Sounds of vibrations carry forth words spoken from within the hearts of many unknown Warriors. Indigenous sections forms pockets of doubt amongst Nations upon Mother Earth's carpet. Within 'Spoken Truth' given to our people, waves of hope vibrate. We give teachings to flow from those words spoken, knowledge, wisdom to encourage Nations to unite and free the waves of sound to enhance the well being of all Nations. Wisdom's growth forms rainbows of pureness from those who wish the teachings to be heard. Bring forth much. Listen Feel through own self the right, the wrong. Understand the true meanings of each. Nations troubles start from within all. Place honour bestowed upon new life. Bring forth teachings to those who wish to nurture and feed from wisdom itself. Many gather to teach. Many falter when teaching through lack of knowledge written through time itself. Place trust when given knowledge from those chosen to walk with me along pathways trodden by many of time past. Within the footsteps, gather pureness of soul. Doorways begin to open when teachings understood. Meaningful messages walk within each word spoken. Listen. Learn and acknowledge the wisdom given. Man itself brings forth blinkers to which the true self hides own truthfulness. Lift the shades of darkness that surround many. Fears of the unknown respect. Shelter from those who wish harm. Give love to those who bring forth own fears. Walk beside those fears with the ones who cross over the line of doubt. Many wish to follow but lack understandings, teachings break free darknesses that surround many. We acknowledge the faith given by those of the home. Teach truth. Begin to surround the followers of many Nations with the teachings and learn to understand all aspects of their chosen walkways. Never doubt, never judge, never force the teachings. Leave bright lights not darkness. Freedom of choice given. Teachings we bring forth many. Understandings and meanings of the words spoken given to those of purity, mind and soul. Understandings begin to flourish from within. Nurture, greed let go. Monetary means will enhance the darkness. Nature's balance comes from within each and every one, only then can teachings mean the forces from which we exist will enhance the very essence of man. We know you know the meaning of love, honesty and truthfulness. Bring to the surface the lightness that was given to you all when life itself began. Mother Nature breathes and feels the pain from which the hurts done by many form shadows within the hearts of many. Release angers, fears, doubts will dwindle once the pureness flows once again within the veins that carry the food of life around each and everyone. We give to all the openness to walk the pathways of pure light to each and everyone. Choose your own destiny by the pureness of the soul.

Judgement gives off vibrations of darkness. Within each vibration given, misunderstandings of the word spoken gathers and prevails to which many follow the footsteps of wrong doing. Each wrong doing causes ripples of darkness to flow throughout the Nations of today. Keeper to those forces of darkness relinquish. Amongst those true believers of the pureness given within the souls of man bring forth the light bestowed upon all. Radiate truthfulness, burn brightly. Forces of darkness dwindle once touched by the true beams of love. Given choices amongst races of many. Winds carry seeds of lightness to within all corners of your world. Give precedence to within own self. Breathe the essence of lightness. Radiate harmony from within. Balance own self and nature will follow. Bring harm to each and harmony crumbles.

23rd October 2005

We give teachings for all to share. Walk free within own shell. Never doubt those whose beliefs bring troubled times. We share sorrows amongst vibrations around your world. Many follow cultures not of own beliefs. Within all cultures vibrational aspects travel far beyond Mother Earth's radiance far beyond all breathable air of your kind. Knowledge written by ancestors of all bring vibrational levels to walk before all. Travellers through time rekindle meanings of Spoken Truths. We share amongst true believers all knowledge and wisdom to begin the walkway of peace. Nations survival of all rests within the heart of those who walk with me. Gifts of light shine strong. Waiver towards the shadow of darkness and peace will shatter once more. Place trust of own wisdom. Gather the fruits of Mother Earth's wisdom. Walk free once more upon the carpets of life itself upon which footsteps form rainbows of energies. Guidance for all to enhance own self. Share wisdom. Open heart to envelop the meaning of harmony. Balance within own thoughts. Teach own self the right from wrong. Undo deeds of anger. Troubled minds cloud much.

24th October 2005

We know we share sorrows of all. Barriers come from within against Nations of war zones. Places burn, crumble to ashes. From the ashes new forms rise once more. Listen to own wisdom, words known. Guidance given to understand own sorrows. Walkways open to many followers of peace and harmony. Tread slow amongst those who show fears. Begin to teach words spoken of true peace and harmony. Gain the trust of those fallen. Bring forth the brightness for which shadows of fear dwindle.

7th November 2005

We gather thoughts from many followers of all Nations around Mother Earth. Each vibrational energy forms ripples of incompletion. Tribal leaders within the Nations walk alone. Many wish to follow footsteps of own Nation. Begin the completion of own walkway to peace amongst the threads of pureness laid down by all of time past. Gather all inner thoughts of peace and share with all who cross over the pathway chosen by own self. Each meaning within the shared words of harmony radiates along the golden threads of past and present. Each spoken word of truth will embed in the heart of many enabling the threads of pureness to flow through energies given out by each and everyone. Place trust and honour in own self's ability to change the way of own life style. Each and everyone who changes but a small amount of selfishness will enhance the growth through balances of harmony. Many words give lasting emotions. In each word, love and lightness stays within. Words of coldness blinker deep within, scars of the mind dwell within. Release the hurts and pain given from such words of coldness. Remember all we say, all we do, has a lasting affect on the small child whose nurturing paves the way for a new life to begin. Offer to those who cross own pathway the hand of peace to enable growth to be shared amongst many. If anger shown, release energies of pureness to surround the one who distorts the vibrational softness of light. Warmth radiates throughout time. Peace loving energies will enhance the true meaning spoken by many for which peacefulness will enter through the openness of the heart of many true followers.

16th November 2005

Time evolves many times through each decade. Truth and honesty teaches trust of many Nations to enhance life's own breath of purity to enable all to walk and share in abundance the gift of all Mother Natures' creations. Bring forth own worth, understandings of life's energies grow from within. Breathe the air of love to begin own journeys. Judgement of doubt clouds much. Clear own fears. Begin and walk each pathway within the brightness of all. Teach own self the balance between all given from when life began. Change not of what is needed change only that of what is understood. Waves of hope gather from many followers of peace.

16th November 2005

Each footstep carries voices from my people to the world of today. Begin to walk upon the pathways open. Share with me the love of all. Cherish not only own beliefs but beliefs of others. Gift of time spent with those who are needy will embed in the hearts of those who wander alone on many pathways. Force not issues of own rights. Believe in all words spoken from all Nations of truth, understandings. Each wave of hope links through times other than your own. Gather thoughts from those who wish to be heard amongst the true followers of peace.

17th November 2005

Pathways give guidance to many. Place trust of those who share the voyage of peace. Walk within the harmony of the soul to enhance the rainbow's brightness that surrounds all who walk upon Mother Earth's carpet. Place own footsteps of purity amongst the leaves of Mother Nature's energies for which golden threads will join and unite along the journey walked by the one of truth and honesty. Peace will enhance Mother Nature's core to enable much to begin to flourish and nourish all to enhance life as it once stood for. Balancing within each and own self radiates vibrations along the golden threads placed down by those of time past. Each golden thread of lightness will begin to vibrate own energies through the veins of sustenance given by Mother Nature's walkways. Time exists for all to share in the reclamation of the hurts done to many. Share amongst own sort the wisdom and courage of own true beliefs. Waiver from the lightness will enhance the shadows that form sorrows. Each cloud of darkness will encase the light that burns deep within. Many who walk amongst the shadows of darkness fail to feel the lightness that burns within all. Shed the doubts and fears. Lift own thoughts of sorrows and pain. Bring forth rays of brightness back to within the home. Search for guidance of those who share the walkway of openness. Gifts of guidance and knowledge we give to all. Amongst many, few we live through. Each Warrior chosen carries the flag of truth and honesty. Place before those chosen the openness to which guidance can be given. Once pathways of choice stepped upon life will begin the journey of fulfillment. Peace will walk beside those who share all wisdom and knowledge of the true meaning of birth for which life begins the growth of new beginnings.

Peace Keepers rise for all Nations. Beliefs of my people will enhance the pathways given to many. We share amongst all the wisdom, the knowledge and the true meanings of all existence given within the sanctity of life itself. Walk amongst the plains of ancient ones for all to be understood. Each pathway opens doorways. Walk amongst many Warriors who wish the true meaning of love and life to be understood. Each passage of words spoken will enable many to reach forward and to undertake the start of new beginnings for which many hope for to bring the love back to humanity. Rocks form pillars. Each pillar formed carries life towards the clear blue skies. Mother Nature's arms surround all living breathing creations for which life is given unconditionally for all to share amongst each and everyone. We bring blessings in the ways of old. Nourishment feeds the soul, wisdom feeds the hearts of many followers. Each breath taken sustains life. Reach fulfilment of inner self. Breathe the pureness once more. Allow fears and doubts to drift from within. Feel, touch the earth beneath own footsteps. Energies from the touch of the hand radiates through the carpet surrounding the earth. Release lightness from within. Walk hand in hand with each other.

Join together and radiate and trust the love we share amongst Nations of today's world.

White Eagle

Whispers Of Wisdom

Wings Surround Many Nations Of Your World.

Place Honour, Trust And Your Beliefs Above Many Thoughts Of

Coldness.

White Eagle

Harmony comes from within. Teach only the truth for wisdom of true beliefs will shine and radiate through the

Openness of those who wish to walk amongst those true followers who walk upon the sands of time. Each footstep placed upon the carpet of

Pureness given from the blessings of Mother Earth's heart. Golden threads line each step trodden to enable all life to continue along each walkway of

Existence.

Brother To All

White Eagle

Peace walk within Mother Earth.

Sands of time follow beside those who believe and walk with me.

Each footprint leaves a mark upon which belief moves slowly within to enhance the balance laid down by all who wish the pureness of peace and harmony to flow freely.

Time itself moves swift amongst Nations of today.

Release all doubts and bring forth a new beginning to enable followers to treasure the gift of Mother Earth's love.

White Eagle

Waters flow deep, take hold.

Child grow strong when feelings of the soul walk beside all Nations followers.

Place heart, soul within lightness and warmth.

Blanket own feelings of worthfulness.

Change life only if need. Bring together love for others.

Walk beside those who cherish the meaning of true worth.

Black Eagle

Many wise words given for the understanding of many ways. In each understanding lies the truth of all. Who knows which walkway of life holds beliefs of trust, honesty, forgiveness, only the one who walks the path of own beliefs who then will change not all but own self. My given teachings is to blame no one but try to understand everyone. Many stories written, enacted for all to share, bring forth only one teaching, deception of honour and trust. My own teachings of time past brought waves of honesty and brightness to share along with many others who walked amongst pain and suffering. Keepers of wisdom walk today amongst the shadows of darkness. Each footstep laid upon the heart of Nature's carpet are placed down with many blessings from the hearts of many Warriors of time past who walked upon the plains of old. All changed only what was given, took only what was needed, gave much of themselves to replenish all enabling all to share plenty. Teachings are given to each and all to begin the understandings of life's struggle, in the hope of many ancient beliefs of all Nations around the world today to balance once more the true meaning of peace and harmony, which will enable life to continue for all to share the beauty of Mother Nature's gift.

White Eagle
24th November 2005

Shimmering lights fall upon transcendent beams

around luminous pockets of pureness.

Each pocket within holds the gift of love.

Treasure own pocket within.

Pureness of the heart shelters no hardness from the seed of life.

Running Bear

Fires burn bright when many teachings of ancient beliefs through stories are told. Each tribe of our people gather knowledge and wisdom through many visions. Our beliefs in the true way of life pass through time. Many of our ways are told to teach the young the true ways of freedom. Teachings are told by Elders amongst my people.

Sacredness of corn is shared to enable life to continue. Each corn picked to feed plenty shares the wisdom taught by ancient ones. Smoke carries words of sacredness to Father Sky. Each offering brings forth messages. Dust of the earth carries on the breath of the winds. Each grain shares through time, knowledge of sacredness of ceremonial dancing. Each beat of the drum, each footstep placed down, has meaning and power to enhance the vibrations to which ancestors acknowledge. Ravens protect when disturbance of sacredness undertaken.

Many wish to close doorways to keep beliefs to within tribal cultures. Bring forth openness. Share amongst all Nations the acknowledgement of our wisdom. Meanings and understandings given once openness shared for all peace to walk strong amongst Nations of today. Peace Keepers of many Nations struggle through darkness to enhance the love to share within the bright lights of pureness. We give many words to teach those who gather who wish the fulfillment and understandings of messages given. Touch the hand of each with the love and understanding of hope.

Chief Dan Evehema
23rd November 2005

Tides turn, waters rush.

Beneath soil life grows.

Nature's forces shine through where darkness shelters.

Life's growth of all creations begins to walk free

once own true beliefs understood.

Chief Sitting Bull

Bring forth new beams of brightness. Walk within shadows no more. Peace to many Nations will rise slowly. Many wishes of peace and harmony bring vibrations to our Realm. Words chosen to enhance the true meaning of life. Honesty of man's wishes will enhance the fulfillment of Nation's trust. Footprints placed upon the carpets of Mother Nature placed down many times when the open plains of my people were free for all to share amongst tribal Nations.

Thunder brought rains for my people to relish the nourishment given by Mother Nature's waters. Keepers of ancient beliefs began stories to rekindle the ways taught by all Elders of time past. Many walked many pathways to gather all knowledge and wisdom to share amongst Nations. Ties broken, many moons passed by. Ways of ancient ones still in the hearts of those who wish peace to flow through the veins of all.

Man's troubles begin from within. Hold within each hand the stone of plenty. Keep only the one that nourishes the wants that is needed. Lay down before own footprint the one chosen to fulfill the needs of own self. Give the hand that carries the one disregarded to the one whose beliefs falter from within.

Many who walk upon pathways of greed lack the knowledge and wisdom passed down by Elders of all Nations. Tribal beliefs of all races stay through time. Open closed doorways to enable wisdom to flow once more through the veins of life. Share amongst own people kindness. Touch many by words of softness. Each pillar of knowledge stands for much. Beliefs of Nations will strengthen foundations of all pillars built when ancient ones walked free upon many plains around the world.

My meaning of the words given to all who wish to walk amongst those of truth and honour is to follow the ones who gathered knowledge and wisdom to enable the homelands of many Nations to flourish. Bring new beginnings to start pathways of pureness, peace and honesty once more for all races to continue with life amongst all colours and creeds.

Distance those beliefs of hurts and angers. The winds of change will carry shadows of fears amongst the vibrations of pureness to dissipate for ever more. Begin the journey and walk towards the bright light that still shines for those who wish for man, woman and child to walk hand in hand and raise the emblem for all to share of love.

Young Male Boy
Aged 12-13 Years
23rd November 2005

Freedom of Spirit

Gather

seeds of love

through windows to our Realm.

Thoughts carry on the breast of Mother Nature's

breezes.

Little Horse

Within all Nations much carries on the wind of Mother Nature's breezes. All thoughts of pureness carries vibrations of lightness for all to share. Love from the hearts of many flow through time as waters carry forth energies of pureness to nourish all who share in the fulfillment of life. Radiate from within the love, the lightness and share with all the pureness of the heart and soul and envelop all who wish to walk the pathway of enlightenment to bring forth the true meanings of peace and harmony. Balance all that surrounds own self to enable the walkways of lightness to carry forth the true meaning of all Spoken Truths.

Many share and acknowledge the meanings of love given by many. Those who challenge the pureness of many who walk upon the pathway of many colours fear own beliefs. Walk beside those, encourage the lightness to surround the ones who walk within shadows. Preach not, teach only from within the understandings and teachings of my people. Place upon those who fear not only that of own doubts but that of what the eye cannot see. Leave words of wisdom upon those who fade from the truth and honesty of many.

Seeds planted from chosen words bring forth saplings. Each sapling will grow from within. Chosen teachings will enable to step from shadows onto the pathway of many colours for which the true being will grow once more. History encourages darkness to flourish. Nature's carpets absorb many sorrows passed through time. Each blanket of darkness covers much of the pains done to many through time. Release own energies to within the pockets of past sorrows. Release own energies of pureness to enhance the lightness which will radiate through time.

Messengers of peace walk through many forms of darkness to enable those who follow in the footsteps to breathe the pureness once more within the energies left for all to share.

Grey Cloud
27th November 2005

Preach no words.

Teach only the truth when given.

REMEMBER,

Hearts fill with pureness when teachings of truth given

Running Wolf

Stories hold many mysteries of time passed. Within each story read by the fires of warmth, teachings are given to those who listen. From all words, Spoken Truth can be felt.

Leaves start to change from the brightness of colours to the darkness of amber gold. As Mother Nature draws winter close, fires start to burn, warmth radiates from the glowing embers, shadows form from the flames that dance from within the heart of the burning fires. Gather together the small child to within the circle of the home. Place the arms of love round each and everyone. Teachings can be heard in many forms. Live through the stories written of time past and present. Radiate and shine the love from within. Share amongst own few within the heart of the home and rekindle within each, the burning candle bestowed within the heart of each newborn to enable all meanings and all beliefs to surround and comfort those who walk within the lightness of Mother Nature's blankets.

Stories of many cultures of the way life once was, will dance through time as the flames from burning coals dance amongst the shadows of every night that falls upon the world of today. Each flame that flickers with the brightness of heat warms the very soul of all life given.

Naiche
27th November 2005

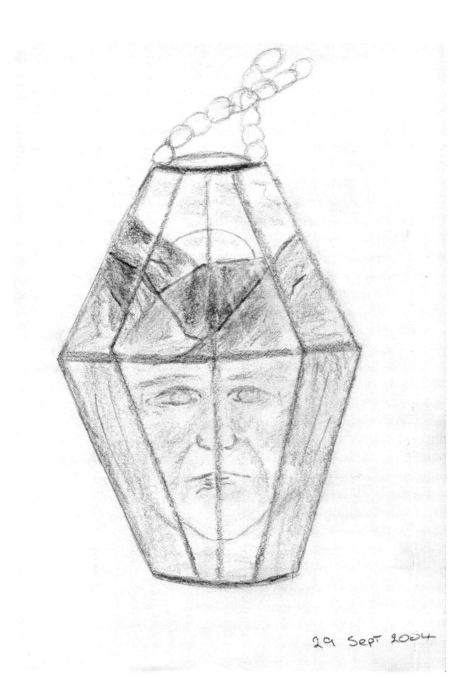

29 Sept 2004

Each force wait.

Pureness of the heart shines strong.

Windows glisten through which our words spoken.

Sands fall upon zones in time.

Nations gather, arms embrace.

Words spoken,

Gift of

LOVE.

White Eagle

Heavenly stars burn bright amongst the darkness of the night. Gather all to share the beauty and harness the fears that flow within as darkness fall upon the earth. Many fears of the unknown are enhanced by the night skies. Sounds of movement within darkness change own beliefs into doubts. Open within own heart, embrace the silent nights that fall when the moon begins to shine. Mother Nature's creations walk silently amongst the shadows of the night. Caress and embrace the love, the energies that fall upon the earth given by the sacredness of the moon's vibrations. Release and vanquish the doubts brought on by fears of the unknown from the shadows that dance and flicker within the glow of the moon. Night falls upon the grounds that are walked upon by many. Each footstep absorbs the powers given by the energies that flow from within.

Many acknowledge the mysteries held within the darkness. Clear own fears, absorb and nourish from the sacredness and pureness of the silver threads given by the powers of the moon. Listen to the songs carried upon the wings of Mother Nature's breezes, songs enhanced by the rays that shine from the hearts of many. Encourage the warmth to flow within. Acknowledge the moon source. Feed own self with the energies and the brightness. Remain untouched by fears of the unknown. Gifts given by those chosen to walk the pathway of peace. Acknowledge the heavenly stars, absorb the warmth of the sun, fear not the darkness, absorb the rays of the moon. Acknowledge all these wondrous gifts of Mother Nature. **PEACE BROTHERS** for all to share amongst all Nations.

Naiche
27th November 2005

Love all who feel through souls window.

Ride the waves of pureness.

Each light fires within.

Gather fuel of the heart to embrace Mother Earth's core.

Chief Sitting Bull

Waves crash upon the shores of time. Each wave carries energies of Nature's forces. Father Sky sheds tears of plenty to nourish the lands and waters that flow across the sacredness of Mother Earth's carpet.

Eagle soars high above watching the lands beneath, calling as each wing beats to the rhythm of a silent drum.

Ravens follow shadows of darkness gathering strength from the soft winds that blow, watching and guiding those who walk within the bright lights of pureness.

Night falls upon the plains. Shadows dance amongst the beams of light offered by the hands of the moon. Wolves howl, not known to man the reason why. Eyes bright, young play amongst the golden leaves burnt by the heat of the sun, sheltered by the wise and given the love shown by all.

Each story to be told by many shares the love and belief of all wisdom passed on through time. Touch those who pass by with the knowledge and understanding. Judge not but offer the hand of love and share a moment in time to listen. A voice heard is a voice shared.

Running Wolf
28th November 2005

Ride the winds of change.

Bring forth new beginnings.

Light fires.

Grow strong. Break bonds.

Nature flourishes.

Geronimo

Droplets of water fall upon many lands. Each raindrop radiates the true beams of life. Each beam glistens with colours shown by the flames given by the sun. Each colour forms the Rainbow Bridge for all to share the glory of Mother Nature's blessings.

Walk beside each and all. Share the glory from beneath own footsteps. Feel from the heart the true beauty of the lands. Give back that which has been taken for many moons. Abundance of life will grow strong. Strength will blossom for man. Each seed sown and nurtured will shed young amongst the sands of time.

Walk amongst the true ways of old, unite, join together. Place beneath the shadows of doubt, the openness to which life shall shine through once beliefs of pureness understood. Rays of bright lights shine from the stars given to walk once more in **PEACE.**

Naiche
28th November 2005

Nature's alliance brings forth lightness for those who wish to walk

the pathways trodden from the one true being.

Walk slow with me towards the Bridge of all Eternity.

White Eagle

Shadows of darkness cloud those who carry the burdens of sorrow. Look for the strength through windows of brightness. Feel from within. Teach own self the understandings of many words spoken. Each deed done by those who reap for self gain, fool only but a few.

Never close doors. Open the heart to enable the flame that dwells within to burn bright once more. Cover no fears with the misunderstandings of time past. Fears form many shadows for which doubt of own self becomes reality. Trust in all spoken from within the heart. Share with all the true ways of trust given.

MY PEACE I share with the true followers who wish to walk upon the lands of plenty once more, to regain the peace broken when truths of many were covered with shadows of darkness.

Geronimo
28th **November 2005**

Gather memories from within.

Search your soul for the true being that dwells within each and all.

Take pity on no one but oneself if truth falters.

HONESTY

begins with the heart and soul of all.

Naiche

My Peace I Share

Kaleidoscope of many colours dance across the midnight skies, within each colour crystals glisten from the lands below. Energies dance within the pyramids formed within the sacred peaks built by Mother Nature's tremors.

Nature's waves flow for all to share amongst Nations of all cultures. Each wave enhances the beauties that surround and covers the earth's nakedness.

Pockets gather the tears shed by Father Sky. Within the pools of water, growth begins to form. Energies vibrate through the ripples formed by the touch of Mother Nature's breezes. Harness the ripple and energies die. Release and give space, each ripple continues to vibrate. Within each vibration energies grow in strength.

My words of wisdom for the words spoken is to understand to harness and abuse Mother Nature's gifts the lands begin to fall and crumple and die within. Release and give back the freedom, Mother Nature's arms of love will replenish for all to share through the times to come.

Aho!

Chief Dan Evehema
28th November 2005

Place songs of joy

upon

those who tread only light footsteps

upon

the walkway to trusting in the belief of others.

White Eagle

Within the clear blue skies soft white clouds begin to form. Within each cloud energies begin to vibrate. Nature's way of clearing and purifying the air that is breathed by all is to shower the rains across the lands laying down the dusts that form through man's creations. Each particle of dust carries and harbours many things to harm all living, breathing creations of the one who walked upon the earth before time was known to man of today. Purification and cleansing of much used by man in the way of life today will enable the veil that surrounds the earth to replenish and to heal all open wounds.

If man ceases to acknowledge the harm of own greed in the use of Nature's resources, life as you know of today will cease to exist in time. Open the heart with the understandings of all words spoken by many.

Black Elk
28th November 2005

Songs gather the pureness of hearts within.

Each told beliefs of pureness.

Gather many for all to share.

Waste not upon shadows of mistrust.

Balance the heart with the gift of love,

Share the warmth from within.

White Eagle

My teaching for you all to share is the beauty for all living creations. Within all pathways, gifts of Mother Earth dwells. Each wondrous gift goes unnoticed to the eye of man.

Walk with ease and share each of Nature's smallest of creatures. Place the hand upon the lands that were once of plenty. Watch for the smallest that walks beside own footsteps. Each giant known as man to the smallest of creatures shares all walkways to enable life to continue and to nourish from Mother Earth's carpets.

Footsteps placed down around all Nations of the world take the life from within every living, breathing creation. Each of the many small creatures that walk amongst the crumbled leaves and grasses feeds the source known to man as earth to enable life to continue. Feel the energies of all existing creations.

Remember to thank within the heart of own self, the abundance of many small but essential beings that give and bring forth the source to which feeds and nourishes all of Nature's branches. These nestle beneath the carpets that surround and hold together the vibrations and energies to which the world of today known to man survives for.

My belief in all creations is the source of energy which sustains life. Each child born to man, woman feeds from inside the womb. Each child feeds from the nourishment given through the wondrous gift of the chord of life. Break the chord of life and each child leaves the warmth and the comfort of the inner sanctity of the Mother's womb. Therefore, teach and give the child born to man the wisdom to gain the knowledge of teachings that have been passed from ancestors of many Nations.

All things are born from within. Seeds sown by the Earth replenishes the source of nourishment for man. Man becomes the source of a seed carrier to fulfill the growth of new life to begin the journeys to fulfill destiny. Each wondrous gift of life shares the joy of Mother Nature's blessings.

White Eagle
29th November 2005

Wings fold around those true followers

of Mother Nature's desire.

Feel the warmth, understand the love given,

give only the truth.

Trust not the desires of greed.

Naiche

Look at the values of what you feel is of importance. Never fool yourself by being of two minds. Choose only the way to which would enhance your way of truth and honesty. Forgiveness is hard to achieve for all. Feel from the heart, look within the deed done, for many answers will be found. Change disappointments of others to understandings of what was given. Leave hurts of unjust to disappear amongst the winds of change. Step on to the path of harmony for which peace of the soul will be found.

Break the bonds of mistrust. Feel the warmth and understandings given by me to make ways for truth, trust and honesty to flow from the veins that sustain all life's forces within each and everyone. Begin to bring forth forgiveness to enable the true way of life to flow freely once more upon the lands of many Nations. Many walk upon pathways of mistrust.

Share the knowledge and wisdom of Wisdom Keepers throughout time. Plenty of words spoken bring fears amongst all Nations. We give honour to those who believe in own true ways. Peace from my people we bring to all in the hope of Mother Earth regaining the energies to sustain all life who walk beneath and upon the blanket that surrounds her bleeding heart.

Many challenge the ways of ancient ones. Many doubt **Spoken Truth** given for all to share. Openness of the heart and hand we bring for you to join together and walk the way of true peace once more.

Chief Sitting Bull
29th November 2005

Time leads to nowhere,

No one follows without a choice.

Give to those only promises of the heart.

Gifts of love given.

Share amongst all the true beliefs of time past,

walk amongst all, share the wisdom given.

Chief Cochise

My Blessings I Give

Candles of life burns from within the sanctity of the soul. Each light shines bright far beyond the rays of the moon. Beams glisten from many of truth and honesty. Fields of promises carry on the mists of time. Each promise shelters only particles of truth.

Many who gaze upon the rivers of doubt become shadows amongst the ripples that fade in the night. Harness the fears and doubts that dwell within, search the mind, body and soul, start to unveil and understand the pains and the hurts that each and everyone harbours within the doorway of the soul. Once meanings of deeds done understood and released upon the wings of Mother Nature's breezes, life itself will shine through once more. The candle which burns deep within each and everyone will burn brightly and share the warmth and love for all eternity.

We share amongst all Nations, ways of our beliefs to enable all to stand tall and become as one. We give many teachings for all to share and radiate our warmth down upon each and everyone.

Running Bear
29th November 2005

Challenge no one but only oneself,

Guide those who bring doubts to the mind.

Cherish pathways shown,

Limit own self wants.

Geronimo

Particles of light become rays of gold upon each who choose to become Warriors of peace. Place own self beyond barriers of greed. Begin to share silence amongst the rush of life. Feel the warmth of the golden light that burns bright amongst the blue coat given by Father Sky. Touch the carpet that Mother Nature lays down before all. Tread slow. Feel the earth beneath each footstep. Share the love of all Nature's gifts. Learn the understanding of life. Shine brightly, leave no pathway in darkness. Shine the light that burns within and walk with me through the valleys of peace.

Never doubt the understandings of many. Listen, learn, take within own self words spoken from many Nations. Beliefs of those who walk amongst the shadows of doubt form pockets of fears. Touch with the love and the warmth of own understandings, preach not my words I bring. Give only own true understandings of the words given by many who wish peace to flourish amongst nature's creations.

Once the cloak of darkness begins to fade, offer the hand of openness to each and everyone. Guide along the pathway of brightness for which the essence of mankind will flow upon the rivers of life. Valleys of darkness begin to shine the bright lights of peace and harmony for all to share.

White Eagle
29th November 2005

Wings of love surround those who walk beside all followers.

Trust Nature's own gift.

Replenish those who walk with fear.

Chief Sitting Bull

Breakwaters crash upon open shores. Many feet walk within the seas of time. Whispers of many Spoken Truths carry upon the winds of change. Gifts from Mother Earth are showered amongst all which are far beyond the understandings of man. Begin to acknowledge the respect given by all creations to enable the life cycle of man to continue through time. Winds move silently, move swiftly, touch each and everyone with the softness that cradles the air that supports life itself. Breathe shallow and life struggles, breathe deep and life gains strength to continue.

We share all life's colours. Each colour brings rainbows of joy. Shade colours of brightness and joy becomes sorrows. Tears of brightness cascade and fall from Father Sky's arm. Within each golden tear drop that cascades from heaven above ripples of peace and harmony begin to form.

Within these words I share with you the joy of my teaching. Breathe the air of life. Touch the waters that flow. Feel from within the true meaning of Mother Earth's gifts so all may continue to walk the plains of old for eternity.

Crows Foot
30th November 2005

Many fall upon broken lands,

Take no wars within.

Enter the light that brings forth brightness to the sorrows and pain

that dwells deep within.

Chief Cochise

Blessings My People, Walk With Me

Child born to man walks within the brightness of many colours. Nations true beliefs gather amongst the waves of hope. Each child born within the love and serenity of pureness walks the pathway of new beginnings. Teach own child the meaning of truthfulness and honesty. Bring all forms of love to enhance the walkway to which each child learns all values of peace and harmony. Many walk within the blue light. Nations of all known to man will bring forth the star of purity. Place the hand of love before all. Nurture and bring the abundance of Nature's gift of peace to walk amongst the child known to my people as child of Indigo. Crystal lights of many shine rainbow beams. Treasure the essence of life, share own beliefs with all.

Mother Nature caresses all, peace given from within the heart of life itself. Understand the true ways of peace and harmony. Gifts of plenty mean nothing, gifts from the heart and soul bring forth the true meanings of warmth, love and understandings. Gains from the worth of nothing leaves pockets of emptiness. Treasures of gold and silver burn from within the shadows of greed The gift of worth taken from the love shared by Mother Earth, fills the heart with joy. Treasure only that of which is given from

within the heart and soul. Grains of sand are worth more than pockets of gold if given with love and warmth from within.

No Name Given
1st December 2005

FLAME OF GLORY FOR
ALL NATIONS WHO
WALK THE PATHWAY
OF PEACE.

WHITE EAGLE

Change no other but each other,

Walk beside all within.

Open the heart of forgiveness to each and everyone,

Judge no one but own self,

Forgiveness comes from within.

Naiche

Peace My Brothers

When winter nights fall many shadows dance amongst the softness of the moon. Share the knowledge and wisdom with many who wish to become as one. Keepers of our ways tell many stories of how life was and how life should be. Within each word spoken follow own visions of the mind to feel and touch the true meanings told by many of time past and present.

Within the warmth of the fires, flames dance like the ghosts of time past. Dampen the fires and shadows fade, warmth disappears and coldness creeps in. Balance the fires of the night, keep the embers glowing, warmth stays to comfort and caress those who share the sacredness of the flame.

Many wish to walk in the arms of peace. Cradle the love offered within words spoken. Change doubts and fears, open the heart, walk within the true flame that burns for all to share.

Life of all becomes a river of greed. Change the heart to only receive what is needed. Spread the arms of love to those who share own doorways and rekindle the flame of glory that burns within.

Many Moons
1st December 2005

Place heart and soul within bright lights,

Surround all you meet within the rays of trust and love.

Honour the beliefs of all Nations.

Give only that of truth and honesty,

Break no promise, offer the hand of openness.

Naiche

My Wisdom I Bring. No Doors Close

Begin to walk amongst the joys and revelations of Nature's beauty. Many wondrous moments in time reveal the true meaning of purity in the heart. Many things evolve within only but a second of time. Sands shift, waters flow, winds change which vibrate the tree that bears the fruits of life. Movement of all through time changes much. Release angers and sorrows to begin the pathway of lightness. Give love and love shall be given. Share a moment in time and memories will exist. Dwell in the shadows of time and darkness will follow. Walk towards the openness of many and bright lights begin to shine. Search for the peace that lies within. Give nothing, nothing shall you receive. Give much and much shall be given.

I share with all who wish peace and harmony my teachings I bring from the heart. Treat those who cross own pathway with the understandings and give only warmth of the heart. Bear no judgment of those who walk under the emblem of misunderstandings. Give off love and love shall be received, give off coldness of the heart and doors will close. The chain of life continues, each link resembles the sands of time. Misunderstandings link through the home. Free all links of coldness and golden threads will join together for all to share in the walkway to come of peace and harmony.

Yellow Hawk
1st December 2005

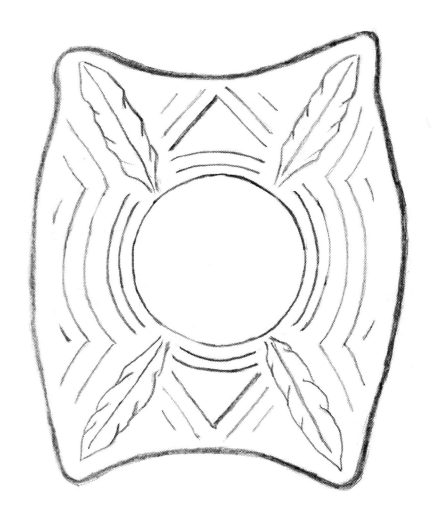

Feathers fall upon sands of old.

Night falls, day dawns, sands shift with the winds of time.

Whispers Of Wisdom

carry on Mother Nature's breezes.

Naiche

Memories Come From The Soul

Hold the banner of hope. Begin to walk the pathways of time. Within the footsteps trodden life of time past is etched upon the grain of sand that lies beneath. Sands change through time leaving only a particle that holds many beliefs. Wisdom grows from within. Each grain of sand passed on through time flows free amongst the winds of change.

In each hand offered from those chosen to bring forth many teachings of wisdom and knowledge, holds the essence of pureness given by many who walk free upon the plains of ancient ones. Teach only the truth. Truth bears all knowledge of existence. Dwell within the shadows that form amongst the doubts and fears of many and truth will be shadowed.

Hear from many the words of my people. Share amongst those who wish to gain the understandings of all teachings. Walk free amongst the beauty of all creations. Live amongst the lightness. Balance between all the true meaning of harmony. Radiate from within the purity of life bestowed upon each and everyone.

PEACE BROTHERS to move free upon the plains of all Nations. Freedom exists to those who choose the walkway of peace and harmony.

Chief Sitting Bull
1st December 2005

Wish for nothing for oneself

but

to wish joy into the hearts of those who wish to

belong.

White Eagle

Clouds form over many Nations. Peace Keeper's walk pathways of old to unite and enhance the walkway of peace and harmony. Walk amongst all creations of Mother Nature. Feel the morning dew beneath own footsteps. Touch the winds that carry on Mother Nature's breath. Sun rises to shine through many silver threads laid down by the eight legged ones. Beneath the earth wings start to open. Breezes form ripples of dust that flow within the arms of ancient plains. Waters dwell within the crevices of time. Many flow in abundance when fed by Father Sky.

Each grain of sand moves swift upon the lands of many Nations covering much of time past, leaving emptiness of time known to man now. Waters once flowed through all Nations with the pureness and sacredness of all existence of life. Cleanse the waters once more by understanding the ways done by man of today. Change own beliefs to walk within the sacredness of Mother Earth's heart.

Many stories share times of old when all walked free amongst all given and shared by me.

Crazy Horse
1st December 2005

Within souls we walk upon your world,

    Enter the doorway with us,

    Trust the hand that guides.

Chief Sitting Bull

Corn grows under the midnight sky, corn fed by the midday sun. Leaves cradle the heart of each cradled in the arms of those who give blessings of Mother Nature's gift. Corn is the very essence of life itself. Each feeds many the sacredness and blessings of our Fathers of many moons past. Each child we teach the meaning of our life source. Reap plenty when peace walk free amongst Nations of my people. Shared within the home are true and honourable teachings. Each corn reaped through time brings forth many blessings of harvest. When seeds grow tall we believe many blessings are to come. When seeds small, darkness will walk free to shadow and darken many walkways of peace. Pureness of the heart falters when seeds die within Mother Nature's breast. Guidance shown to Keepers of each corner to replenish and nourish the earth ready to receive new growth. Many with hold angers. Such angers release shadows of coldness. These shadows walk upon the soils of planting. Each stone that lies beneath the soil of Mother Earth's carpet of abundance feeds upon the energies of pureness or darkness. Release the shadows that fall upon the earth. Give back the lightness once shared by many of past times. Relight the growth of each corn seed planted. Give blessings of lightness to enhance the growth of plenty.

My words spoken - teach to those who wish to listen. **Teach** only, not preach for preaching is not of our ways. My name known to many Peace Keepers, **Brother** to many Nations. Feathers I give to all. **My peace** runs through the veins of each.

White Eagle
1st December 2005

Walk of Silent Footsteps

We give love to those who believe,

Break the bonds of mistrust,

Enter the road to freedom,

Walk beside each other.

Chief Cochise

Offer The Hand Of Openness, Share And Unite

Many bright lights shine from the darkness of the night. Each sparkle that glistens from the skies above burns bright for all to share. Rays offered by the heart of the moon paves the way of many walkways to step upon. Each walkway chosen within the sacredness of own beliefs will grow and shine for many to follow.

Many dance amongst the shadows of the night. Shadows move swiftly and dance with the rays of the moon. Flames flicker and move silently as the winds of time breathe warmth amongst all who share the serenity of the night. **My peace** I share with those who wish all who walk under the true belief of peace and harmony to enable the freedom of love to flow amongst the waves of life.

Many ways of time past share the joy of freedom once given by Fathers of my people. Waste of peace walks free amongst people of today. Many harbour troubles passed on through time. Peace will only walk free once more when simple things are remembered. Each small deed of pureness offered to one or many people shows the way forward to enable the child of tomorrow to relent past misgivings. Honour the ways through life to succeed through small deeds done under the emblem to which all life begins.

Many walk within the darkest of shadows through the beliefs passed on from each of ones own walkway chosen by one who gave life from within the family home. Shelter no judgement. Judgement shown by many of time past. Peace dwindles once judgement is given. Many fall under the judgement of others. Arrows of time past penetrate deep within the heart and soul of my people.

Peace of our Fathers shines from far beyond man's vision of today. Each Warrior passed on through time shares the knowledge and wisdom and understandings written in many of our stories.

Peace Keeper's who walk amongst the world of today holds many feathers of honour. Share the wisdom and the knowledge of those who are the Keepers of today of all wisdom of peace and harmony. Teachings of my Fathers go hand in hand in the hope of freedom to ride the winds as many Warriors rode upon the plains.

My gift of my understandings to share with you - acknowledge all who wish to run like the wind upon the carpet of pureness. **A Brother to many** is all that is needed.

Ho Hay
2nd **December 2005**

Place all beneath Spoken Truth.

Love, lightness, harmony brings forth

Peace.

Balance the way of own heart,

Walk in peace upon the carpet of life given with the love of

Mother Earth's blessing.

White Eagle

Teach the child to be - Stories of all Nations share the ways of peace. True beliefs come from the heart. Walk the journey hand in hand to share the wisdom taught by many. Storytellers of old nurtured many along the walkways of honour. Share with me my ways of life that could once more be. Bring together for all to share the ways of pureness of Mother Earth's precious gifts.

Once the lands were rich for each to walk upon, plenty to share for all to feed and to shelter from the winds of coldness. Many people shared, along with buffalo, the beauty of all freedom. Winds of change blew through our Nations, freedom for all gone like the shadows that dance in the moonlight. Many fought the winds of change. Acceptance to much was feared by all. Nations that we were, were no more.

My teaching to share with you all – never let lie stories from the heart. Leave only sorrows behind. Bring forth joy, share much. Hold open the door from which memories unfold. Fill the home once more with laughter. Radiate the warmth and love from within. Memories are filled with much love to share.

No Name Given
5th December 2005

Shimmers of light gather

small pockets of

hope.

Hope becomes reality once

Spoken Truth given by many

Becomes understood.

Naiche

Peace

Many changes walk beside all. Waste not the chance to walk free amongst the soft winds that blow. Breezes move swiftly upon many plains of today. Each footstep trodden along the pathways of life teaches many to feel for others who not only fail to hear the soft winds that blow, but shelter themselves from the beauty of all that surrounds each and everyone. Many falter before own eyes. Open to see, feel and gain the wisdom that filters from the essence of Nature's blessings.

Many seeds carry on the winds of time sown by many who nurture and caress the soils to enrich the growth of the stem that supports the grain that many will share to fulfill the mind, body and soul of life itself.

My part given for many to share - Walk free as once did many. My Father, my Brothers, now me tell words spoken given by my soul.

Aho!

Taza
Son Of Chief Cochise
Brother To My People, Strong When Given Life.
6th December 2005

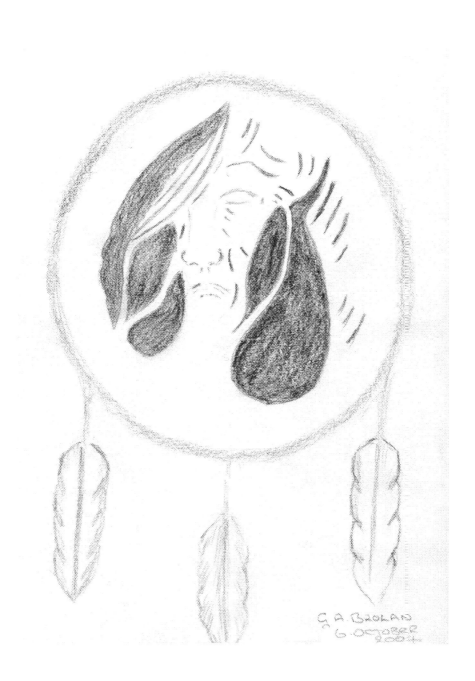

Preach not words spoken.

Take beneath wings of **love**.

Cherish, nourish and grow within.

Geronimo

Sun falls behind shadows of the night. Each shadow shelters the rays that glow with warmth. Sleep settles and rests through the lands. Many move silently upon the cloud of wisdom. Touched by the openness, teachings of the heart radiate from within the rays of the moon. Nights drift by. Mother Earth begins to wake opening the arms of love. The warmth begins to glow from within the flames of the sun. Within the minds of those who shared the cloud of wisdom, knowledge begins to grow from within. The warmth of the sun brings forth many blessings to which life of the newborn begins the first steps of trust. Nurture the ones whose footsteps are small upon the grains of sands that move silently as the breezes blow amongst the leaves that fall from the tree of life.

Many waters flow beneath the soils of Mother Earth's carpet. Within, each droplet that is carried along by the ripples of the waters flowing, brings life for all to share amongst Nature's creations. Lands die through lack of understandings by all, not one but many share in the destruction of Mother Nature's precious gifts. Sun burns dry the waters that were once plentiful. Aridness becomes plentiful not the lush growth of grasses that once moved amongst the winds of plenty. Night skies form shadows of darkness, coldness seeps through the rays once given by the warmth of the dying sun. Many changes seep through the hearts of all Nations. Sow the seeds of harmony and balance once more the gift of life so that each raindrop of water released by Father Sky's tears will fall upon the dusts that cover Mother Earth's blanket.

Chief Cochise
6th December 2005

Nations cold beneath walkways of peace.

Honour bestowed upon chosen followers of our beliefs.

Peace, Thunderbirds reign once more.

Bring truth to many.

PEACE.

Brothers, Sisters, all white, red believers soon gather under peace.

Geronimo

Walk within the rays of the sun. Dance within the shadows that light the night skies. Move freely upon the plains of your Nation. Tread slow. Feel beneath own footsteps the warmth and the love shared by Mother Earth.

Give knowledge to those who wish to share the understandings of the moon, the sun, the earth, the waters that flow amongst the rocks of time. Feel the warmth, the coldness of the winds that blow through the seasons that change with time. Gifts shared by many bestowed upon the lands enriched by Mother Earth's essence, enhances Mother Earth's heartbeat to dwindle.

Take not the crystals that form within each of the peaks that covers the brightness and pureness for which greed takes hold and changes formations of Mother Nature's offerings. Within the heart of each sacred peak burns the life force of the lands that surround the vibrations given by the crystals of ancient blessings. Within each crystal formed by Father Time, many vibrations sleep within the folds of growth.

Nature caresses the pureness to which lands of time past and of time now, feeds from the essence of pureness which radiates through the veins of Mother Earth's life force. Once broken and taken from within the heart of the carrier, all energies that seep through the lands enhanced by each vibration given off by the pureness of each crystal, begins to radiate the pain and sorrows that are carried upon the winds of time now.

Change the need of show. Give back what has been taken by giving a piece of Mother Earth's gift back to within each hole made by time. Place but one thought. Thoughts carry far beyond the senses of man today. Heal from within by own thoughts to cover the wounds done by man.

Each thought given by pureness will enhance the repair and the vibrations of Mother Earth's wounds.

Naiche

Son Of Chief Cochise

Brother To My People, Strong When Given Life.
6th December 2005

Lightness brings forth pureness within wanderers through darkest
doorways. No more enter beneath shadows of long past.
Gather all peoples' wishes to enlightenment
within the reach of each and everyone.

Mohawk

Eagle soars high above the lands of old. Wings of strength beat upon the warmth of the winds of time. Eyes bright for all to see. Many believe and share in the sacredness of the eagle. Feathers fall from the skies above, given to use within the sacredness of many prayers. Offer the prayer of peace to carry on the breath of Mother Nature's breezes. Each wind carries many thoughts. Each thought of pureness settles within the arms of Mother Nature's body.

Vibrations soften the strength of harm, heals the openness of wounds done by man. Caress each vibration given, walk amongst no shadows of doubt, clear own thoughts of fear, allow the pureness of love to each and everyone to flow through the heart and soul and peace will envelop once more.

Feel strong, give the strength that dwells within. Join and unite the vibrations of man to begin the journey of peace with many.

Ho Hay
7th December 2005

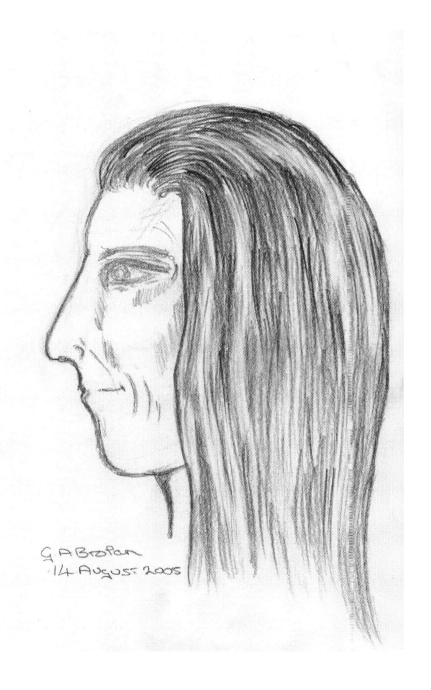

Beneath moon rays,

trust holds back the darkness

from which true believers of our Realm

reaches through corridors of which we share teachings,

meanings and understandings of our work,

to help in the truth of all **TRUST**.

Redeemer Of All – Black Elk

Moon beams travel from Nation to Nation, walkways of golden light radiates from within. Messengers of peace shines the light of truth, each light shines bright for all to share. Open the heart and share the pureness of many teachings. Follow own beliefs. Trust the truth given. Within the lights of many of time past, peace we offer for all to share in the harmony of truthfulness. Many waters flow within each Nation. Tides give guidance to the waters. Within each ripple seen by man, vibrations enhance the creation of life that dwells beneath. Pureness of the waters give pureness of the soul. Each drop taken within own self, treasure the gift bestowed upon the lands. Drink from the waters given and shared by Mother Earth's creations. Feel from within the coolness and the pureness of time past. Touch the earth. Give thanks for all you share. Nature's way of receiving the vibrations of thanks is to replenish and to give back the gift of plenty.

Each pathway trodden upon the walkway of life offers humble but meaningful knowledge and wisdom to share with all the beauty and the gift offered to enhance the way of life. My peace and understandings I share amongst those who walk along the beauty of colours given to mark the pathway open for many. Colours of peace shine above Nations of many enhanced by the waters shed from Father Sky. Each raindrop unites and joins together for peace. Walk beside and join together the hands offered by those true believers of peace and harmony. The hand offered is the hand of many colours.

Chief Dan Evehema
7th December 2005

Reach self esteem by courage of own.

Nations mock me.

Me Warrior.

Brothers to all, walk in peace.

Crazy Horse

Walk within the footsteps of time. Each trodden footstep paves the way for all truth and honesty to bring forth the fulfilment of time to be. Many walk upon coldness of the heart. Each golden ray given by the warmth of the sun brings forth the brightness of how life should be. Clouds form from within, casts doubts amongst fears of shallowness. Each cloud that cloaks the one of misbeliefs forms visions of own terrors.

Take upon oneself and enhance the warmth and the lightness shown by the rays of pureness - offered by Nature's creations will pave the way of own golden footsteps to which many will caress and nourish from the warmth shown. Beliefs of many share the knowledge and understandings of love. Life begins to form rainbows of brightness for which truth of the heart grows from within.

My words spoken are given to enable those of mistrust and beliefs of own greeds, to turn the forces of coldness into the brightness we all wish to share amongst those who walk within the dark shadows of formality.

White Eagle
8th December 2005

Increase the flow of thoughts

to within the purity of the

heart.

Bring forth energies to walk within the sanctity of the

soul.

Peace Brothers.

Naiche

Lights glimmer through silence of the night. Shadows dance like the flames of burning fires. Whispers carry upon the warm winds reaching many who wish to listen. Each voice tells stories of ancient times. Listen to the songs that seep from the mountains that stand tall against the darkness of the night. Feel the earth beneath own feet, vibrations tremor from Mother Earth's heart. Lay the hand upon the waters that give the meaning of life to all. Stand and embrace the warmth shared with you by Nature's breezes. Caress and breathe the air that cannot be seen but is shared by all for life to exist.

Walk amongst the gifts offered by Mother Earth's openness. Break free from bonds of coldness, enjoy the life that has been given, share all that is understood from within the heart. Never harm those that misunderstand the true meaning and belief of Mother Nature's gift.

Blessings I share with all. Words spoken by me bring forth the gift of love and true meaning of life.

Take from the lands the hearts of these, life for all will be no more to share. Give what is needed back to the earth for all to share. Is life itself really so hard to bear?

Standing Bear
8th December 2005

Basic Instincts - Revival

Strive for the pathway of harmony.

Change nothing but oneself.

Radiate love freely.

Nurture growth of peace from within.

Grey Cloud

Many colours change by the warmth of the sun. Many rays dance and beat upon the leaves of green. Colours of gold radiate from above giving life and warmth to enable growth to begin to flourish. Once the warmth dies from within the skies, coldness settles upon the carpets that cover the plains of many. Many believe in the ways told by the Wisdom Keeper's of old.

Night falls, many rise and ride the plains of old. Keepers of many stories tell of forefathers who rode as swift as the winds upon the plains of plenty, keeping watch for those who would come and take from many.

Within the silence of the night wolves howled warning of dangers from within the shadows cast by the night skies. Each howl carried on the winds, another to share by calling from high in the hills. We share many times, many reasons for nature's voices, the raven, the hawk, the eagle, the buffalo and many, many more. Each walked the sacredness of many blessings. Totems given to those see'rs, visionary totems.

Those who walked with the hands that trembled gave blessings to move free amongst many. Each fall of the feather gave way to peace for one feather dropped amongst Tribal Nations, see'r walked amongst followers. Man gave way to peace for then Warrior walked to redeem feather. Once feather given back storms continued.

Many, many teachings can be heard by those of old. Keepers of our ways wish to tell those who listen. Each story given from the hearts of many. Beliefs is of your choosing. Choose the wisdom learnt by own self. Never doubt beliefs of other races. Each believe in own ways. Many ways to which cause doubts amongst other beliefs causes troubled minds through lack of understandings.

Growth of peace depends on those who wish freedom to walk amongst many colours, creeds of many Nations. Offer the hand to which shows the trust and not of judgement. Piece together all words spoken from the hearts of many ancient ones. Take all or just one word given and begin the walk of peace towards the Rainbow Bridge to eternity.

Black Elk
8th December 2005

Circle of Truth

Balance truth amongst own self, give all of your self when need.

Peace follows each footstep of purity.

Harmony will shine through openness.

Chief Sitting Bull

Many walk beside the fool. Follow the one who walks alone. Listen, fear not the words given, fear the one who fools. Many walk between the given choice. Begin to understand the truth between the fool of misunderstanding. Seek own self, begin to walk within the beliefs of choice. Each given choice chosen, believe in. Take that from which doubt clouds judgement.

Understandings will become reality once doubts understood. Never leave open the heart of coldness, clear own fears from within. Feel the love and warmth offered by the unseen hand of Mother Earth. Cherish all that is given, believe in own truths, never waiver from the pathway of righteousness.

Many wise teachings given to all. Take only of that which is understood, leave shadows of doubt. We share many ways with all Nations, guidance given to those who walk within the harmony of life. Balance within own self the truth of all existence. Radiate all truth, honesty from own belief. Within time Nature's blessings will walk free upon the given pathway of pureness.

Crows Foot
10th December 2005

Count the stars within the bright lights of humanity.

Power becomes the source of forgetfulness.

Lift own heart to within the rays formed by wondrous visions.

Naiche

Joy Becomes Reality

Left and right are the hands of life. Open the hands to the warmth of the sun. Close the hands, shadows dwell within. Offer only but one hand, judgement is given. Offer two, openness is given. Reach for Father Sky, the hands offer pureness. Keep hands by the side, shadows of doubt begin to show. Within these words spoken feel the true meaning of what I have shared.

Cradle the newborn child within the arms of love, the hand caresses and warmth is given. Lay the child amongst coldness itself, touched only by the coverings given to keep warm, warmth is shadowed and the touch of love will not be.

Many ways to share the warmth, the love and understandings of all life's creations shines through when true beliefs are given from the heart.

Black Elk
12th December 2005

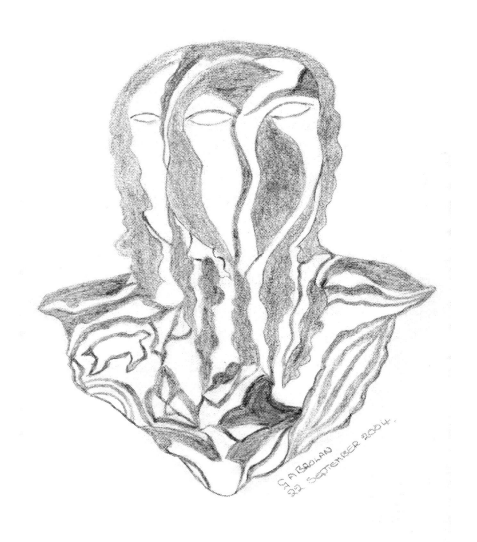

Walk within each arc of brightness,

growth begins to flourish.

Wealth holds meaningless goals

within those who tread coldness beneath own footsteps.

Naiche

Passages in time walk free amongst Nations of old. Each walkway gives birth to new beginnings. Place the arm of forgiveness upon the ones who wrong own beliefs. Guidance from many given to realign pathways of honesty. Below the waters of many seas, life's shadows begin to form within the darkness that dwells below the shell that covers the warmth of Mother Earth's bleeding heart.

Cherish the life given. Walk within the peace bestowed within each and everyone cradled with the arms of the precious gift of life. Many who walk beside the ones who share the rainbow colours of eternity, envelop the true balance of purity. Those who walk beside own self and others of greed and coldness share only the shadows of darkness. Bring to within the home the love, forgiveness and honesty. Shine the rays of warmth within to envelop each cloud of judgement. Bring together the warmth and brightness of life.

Share amongst many the fragrances of harmony shared by many wondrous gifts given by Nature's blessing. Each flower forms new life when the warmth from the sun rays touch and caress the blooms of many colours. Feel the vibrations and energies given off by the life of Mother Nature's creations. Colours of the rainbow enhances the walkways of many truths. Take away the brightness of all creations and life becomes the shadows of darkness.

My teaching I share with all is to live life with colour and harbour only the softness we share amongst the walkways of peacefulness and share with the winds of change the balance to begin the trail of peace. Walk amongst the pathways of darkness and the trail of peace will once more become the Trail Of Tears.

Blessings come from all those who walked upon the plains of old. I walk amongst those who wish to share the joys of laughter, peace and harmony.

Keeper Of Ancient Wisdom
13th December 2005

Waters flow beneath songs of the winds.

Each breeze gathers sounds of many.

Listen, feel the warmth given,

touch with many the hand of those shadowed by

doubts and fears.

No Name Given

Laughter brings joy to the heart. Each tear of joy falls like golden raindrops glistening through the iridescence of the soul. Sorrows dwell beneath the blanket of darkness. Tears of joy replace tears of sorrows.

Gateways open for many who wish to walk in peace amongst the joys shared by Mother Nature's child. Each child born brings joy amongst those who share in the beginning of new life. Caress the hand open by those who walk the pathway of peace. Hold the hand of love offered by the child born to man, joy known only to the hand of child. Share the love, the wisdom to bring peace.

Show no coldness for coldness brings forth sorrows to within the walls of the heart. Man's fears forms clouds of doubt. Doubt brings forth darkness to which the child of purity fears not. Give laughter, laughter shall be given. Share the grief and sorrows form deep within. Shine the beam of love for the child will follow. Show only darkness, coldness will caress the child to be.

Give only the truth to those who listen. Trust own self before trusting others. Give own self to those who wish to learn. Teachings and understandings walk beside those who walk in the footsteps of the one true being of all time.

Piece together that of which is understood. Live life and fulfill own thoughts. Give and not wish to receive, for each deed done to those who have nothing will remain in the hearts of those who suffer the pains of sadness. A gift of little is a gift of plenty. Begin to understand the meanings of many words spoken throughout the teachings given by many. Grains of sand glisten upon the shores of time. Tears of joy feed the hearts of pureness. The hand of love remains solid within the hearts of those touched. Begin to share the joys that surround the child of tomorrow. Heal own self from within. Begin to heal others with the words of peace.

Unite and begin to walk upon the bridge of many colours to enhance and share the new life to come.

Running Bear
13th **December 2005**

Beneath the folds of life shadows dwell deep within.

Clear own thoughts of darkness,

walk in peace.

Share the knowledge and wisdom we bring

for all to walk upon the pathways of

trust and honesty.

Crows Foot

Tenderness of woman's caress seeps through the veins of life. Softness of child's laughter fills the soul with joy. Everlasting love moves deep within.

Shadows of darkness walk amongst many Nations. Fears dwell deep within. Tears of sorrow feeds the shadows of coldness.

Walk within the warmth of the rays offered by the glow given by the sun. Give blessings as each day dawns. Webs of silver threads glisten with the dews given by the darkness of the night. Soft breezes touch the morning air gently shifting the leaves that cover Mother Earth's carpet, Nature's way of giving the love offered for all to share. Peace brings forth bright colours that shimmer and dance, lit by the sacredness of the moon. Cast no doubt of fears to walk amongst the shadows that dance upon the lands lit by the rays of the moon.

Understand the gift we share amongst all Nations. Colour of the skin bears no meaning of the warmth and love offered by each and every one who speaks the words of truth, and trust. Leave open the gateways of life to walk amongst the gift offered of peace and harmony by Mother Earth.

Share each and all of Nature's creations. Bring laughter back to within the darkest hours. Shelter no more sorrows and pain. Begin to share life as one. Walk with me to the beat of my drum.

Chief Sitting Bull
14th December 2005

Blankets warm the body,

Wisdom

feeds the soul.

Share amongst many,

For each will become whole.

Peace I bring to all.

White Cloud

Rains fall upon many plains, given the waters to feed the springs that dwell deep within the heart of Mother Earth's shell. Waste not the gift of life. Fulfill own thirst with the essence of pureness.

Feed the heart of wisdom. Acknowledge the truth of own self. Give to those who share the pureness knowledge of our teachings, and show the way of mankind to enable each and everyone to bring forth the bright lights once more that dwindle within many. Footsteps placed down by those who wish life to begin the journey of peace glisten by the golden threads of forgiveness.

Offer the hand to those who fear many things that the eye fails to see. Guidance given by chosen words will vibrate the energies of peace. Gifts of many teachings will share in the balance and fulfillment of Nature's wishes. Strength of one is strength of many. Choose only the wise not that of the one who shows greed of wealth. Fools follow greed. Only the wise gives back plenty.

Shelter the child that offers the hand of love. Teachings given to enable child to grow strong with the words shared by many. The gift of love strengthens the soul. Peace grows from within. Happiness radiates from the smiles given by the child of love. Cherish honesty and fulfillment will be given.

Chief Cochise
14th December 2005

Precious words come from the heart,

Take all within and treasure the moments you share together.

Within each moment, share all memories of **peace**.

Together unite all within the home.

No Name Given

Give only that from the heart. Feel love of own self before love from others is understood. Waters glisten with the rays of the sun. Warmth moves with the flow of time. Nations walk within the fires of sorrow. Keepers of my people share knowledge given to walk within peace. Thunderbirds gather amongst Nations of old, peace for all to share. Change clouds of doubt, radiate from within the joy and love to bring forth warmth and pureness.

Cherish the arms of Mother Nature's blessings, gifts given to share and walk within the heartbeat of all creations of beauty. Shadows hide many truths, speak many words of wisdom. Understandings of much will call upon the beliefs carried through time on the wings of messengers of peace. Challenge not of coldness, give understandings to much. Teach only from the heart words spoken of peace, trust, truth and harmony. Fears of Spoken Truth forms blankets of coldness. Touch each and everyone with the words spoken by many. Softness of the heart give.

Teach the blessings we share with those who wish to walk amongst the Rainbow Warriors of today. Peace Keepers of time past wish only to bring forth meaningful messages, to enable all to share the love and peace and radiate the joy that once walked amongst many.

Blessings to each and everyone!

Crazy Horse
16th December 2005

Within whirlpools, glistens hope.

Within ripples Nations flourish.

Still waters, dormancy dwells.

Crazy Horse

Happiness brings the joy of love. Many touch the heart to bear pain of others. Teach only the truth. Pathways of many teachings give guidance to enable changes to grow upon the walkways of peace. Open the heart, bring forth harmony. Tears, not of sorrow but tears of joy gives life through meaning of existence.

Child walks within the shadows of man. Teach peace. Balance the child to bring forth harmony. Show joy not anger. Understand the ways of old. Walk hand in hand. Guide the heart of child to believe in own worth. Never leave fears of doubt to dwell upon the child of new beginnings. Born within many, gift of blue light. Peace Keepers to be will walk free amongst Nations. Share the light of brightness and heal Mother Earth's bleeding heart from deeds done by many. Offer the love back. Unite and share once more, all of pureness.

Kicking Horse
16th December 2005

Buds blossom, leaves flourish.

Nature feeds all creations

with the love and pureness of the essence given from within.

Crazy Hawk

Night falls upon the walkways of time. Windows darken, night lights burn bright. Shadows dart between moonbeams of silver. Many teach around fires that burn with the flames of yellows and reds. Each story told holds the mysteries of time. Many child listens with the openness of innocence. Teachings given to learn each child ways of all beliefs.

Each morning rises with the sounds of time. Hear the soft winds which move swiftly across the lands. Cries of many can still be heard through the echoes carried upon the shifting sands. Laughter fades amongst the shadows that form beneath the coldness brought in by the hearts filled with pain.

Place open the hand to the stranger who passes by. Lift the veil of darkness and regain the joy of laughter to share with the one who walks as a stranger. Who knows who that might be? It could be you or it could be me!

Chief Sitting Bull
16th December 2005

Kaleidoscope of lightness burns bright from each walkway of

love.

Breathe the essence of pureness

given by the diamonds of lightness to enhance

The True Being.

No Name Given

Touch each veil of darkness with the golden hand of light. Walk amongst those of misunderstanding with the glistening threads of love. Each footstep placed down amongst that of doubt opens gateways for many to begin the journey of trust.

Many Nations walk the pathways of time searching for peace and harmony but fail to find. Turn around, look at own self for peace and harmony can be found from within. Start the journey forward with the footsteps of time. Place each one down and share with all the joy of love, and peace and harmony will be found.

Crazy Hawk
16th December 2005

Covenant broken, justice prevails.

Redeem all wrongs, forgiveness given.

No Name Given

Each flame burns from the torch of life, burning gold with the essence of pureness which surrounds the child to be. Guidance given for all to share, teachings offered by many. Listen from the heart, take the words of wisdom. Leave not the shadow of doubt to dwell within. Keepers of many rainbow colours walk within the brightness to share with all the love, the peace and harmony to enhance the true way of life.

Understandings differ from Nation to Nation. Beliefs of many change with colour. Hear all words given, speak only the truth. Choices given. Choose wisely the pathway of brightness. Choose only for one self and walk the pathway of loneliness where shadows form amongst the colours of greed. Walk amongst those who wish to hear words spoken of ways of old.

Understandings and meanings given to teach the truth for many to share, and to bring forth the balance and harmony and walk with peace.

Black Elk
16th December 2005

Rivers flow strong.

Strength forces Mother Nature's balance and harmony

to within the unity of life.

Crows Foot

Waters of many oceans are left divided by the hand of all Nations. Waves crash upon the lands of time shifting the stones that glisten with softness. Move close, listen, hear the waves beat upon the shores as whispers echo upon stones of old. Silence of Nature's winds smooth the waters and calm the sands that dwell deep within. Feel the warmth upon the skin touched by the waters of our ancient lands.

Time moves silently. Only man's ways show each mark of the day. The bright glow from each star of the night paves the way to walk the journey forward. The sun, the moon, offers guidance for those to share. A mark in time leaves no passageway open. The mind carries memories to hold close to the heart.

We give teachings to embrace and to pave your way to walk within the light and to carry forward for another day.

Running Bear
17th December 2005

Shards of brightness falls upon all Nations.

Each raindrop gives life to Mother Earth's core.

Waves of hope are carried on the winds of time.

Sands shift, footprints last.

Yellow Hawk

Each walkway through time etched by many footsteps laid down by Nations of past offer the hand of hope to begin the journey of pureness. Envelop peace and harmony to embrace the lands of Mother Nature's blessings. Open doorways to new beginnings. Shine the light for the child of tomorrow. Share knowledge of times past with those who wish to walk free amongst the lands that were once of plenty.

Time moves with the breath of the moon. Child grows once life given. Share the lightness of true belief. Give guidance. Walk the pathway by holding the hand. Caress and nurture, hold deep within. The love from the child for life shall once more begin.

My words spoken I give to share amongst those of new beginnings. Learn only from that what is understood. Teachings of much given from within my heart and soul. Walk in peace, tread slow amongst many valleys of darkness. Learn the words I share to walk hand in hand amongst those who dwell within the shadows of mistrust.

Chief Cochise
17th December 2005

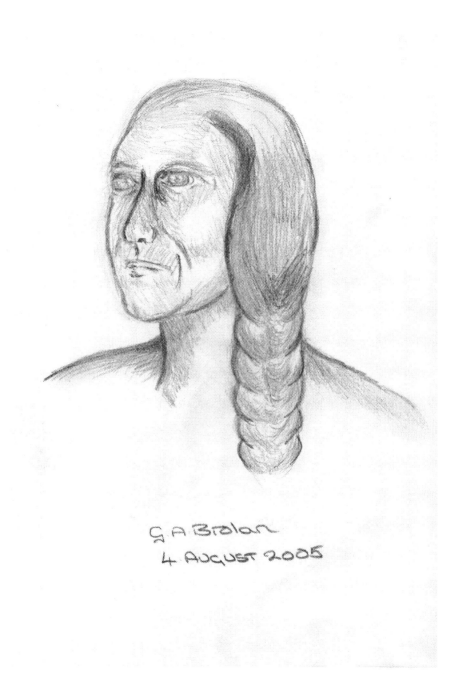

Pools of light radiate through the magnetism of energies shared by reality.

Harmony gathers fulfillment of the mind's eye.

Within the thought process of many,

begin and allow ones own journey forward to evolve within the pureness of the true meaning of life and love for others.

Crows Foot

Walk beside the truth given to share the beliefs of many. Choose words to bring forth understandings to allow own walkways to open. Amongst those who talk speeches of trust, honour and truth, few believe own spoken words. Honour the trust between those who share all spoken words of lightness.

Never shadow thoughts of pureness with doubts of own fears. Brightness walks within many corridors of life. Each ray of hope given by own self radiates far beyond the shadows of mistrust. Balance the harmony of own being. Walk within the gift of life. Change not all but own self.

Peace.

Black Elk
2nd **January 2006**

Messenger of Peace

Place the hand of trust

amongst the ones who walk within the shadows of doubt.

Never judge

those whose beliefs stray from the pathways of righteousness.

Many follow shadows of own fears.

Place within the heart of each the love, the lightness and the

honour of own honours.

White Eagle

Place the hand of lightness upon those who walk amongst shadows of coldness. Place the arm of love around the one who cries tears of sorrow. Gift of pureness flows from within the veins of those chosen to walk the pathways of old. Harmony, balance and trust challenges shadows of misgivings amongst many Nations. Guidance given for all to share. Wisdom of many teachings follow own true beliefs. Hope gives openings for words of wisdom to flow through time.

Begin to walk upon the pathway of peace. Understand the true meanings offered by many who wish for all to share the joy that harmony can bring. Fall amongst the shadows of doubt, fears wrap arms of coldness around the walls that carry the true flame of life. Feed upon the joys given by Mother Nature's blessings. Treasure that what is given, take only what is needed, leave what is not for others to share the gift given by the warmth and love of all nature's creations. Feel the serenity of life once many words of my people understood.

My peace I share amongst those who wish to bring balance back to within Mother Nature's heartbeat.

No Name Given
2nd January 2006

My wisdom I bring to you.

The gift of love I share amongst all Nations.

Raindrops glisten and fall upon the wondrous gift laid down upon the blanket of life that surrounds the heart and soul of Mother Earth's deepest sanctity of honour.

Walk beside each and everyone.

Shelter no anger.

Peace my Brothers and Sisters of all creeds.

Blessings I bring to each and everyone.

White Eagle
5th January 2006

My hand I offer

to touch those who walk within shadows of

doubts, pain and fear.

My hand I give in guidance.

The hand that shows openness bears no judgement.

I give, within the openness of my belief,

knowledge within teachings of wisdom to share amongst those who

wish to walk the roadway of new beginnings

and bring forth to within the home

of each and everyone the true meaning

of what life has to give.

PEACE

White Eagle
5th January 2006

NATIONS WILL RIDE THE WAVES

WITH SMILES

ONCE UNDERSTANDINGS OF ALL TEACHNGS

OFFERED TO SHARE AMONGST

NATIONS OF TODAY

Lightning Source UK Ltd.
Milton Keynes UK
UKOW03f0701140314

228137UK00002B/178/A